Philosophy of Education
since Mid-Century

Philosophy of Education since Mid-Century

Jonas F. Soltis, Editor

Teachers College, Columbia University

Teachers College, Columbia University
New York and London 1981

Published by Teachers College Press, 1234 Amsterdam Avenue, New York, N.Y. 10027

Library of Congress Cataloging in Publication Data

Main entry under title:

Philosophy of education since mid-century.

   Originally published as: Teachers College
record. Vol. 81, no. 2 (winter 1979)
   Includes index.
   1. Education—Philosophy—History—20th
century—Addresses, essays. lectures.   I.   Soltis,
Jonas F.   II.   Teachers College record.
LB41.P579   370'.1   81-780
ISBN 0-8077-2651-6   AACR2

Manufactured in the United States of America

86   85   84   83   82   81   1   2   3   4   5   6

Contents

Contributors

HARRY S. BROUDY is emeritus professor of philosophy of education at the University of Illinois at Urbana. His recent writings have been concerned with the uses of schooling, a new rationale for general education, and the importance of the aesthetic components of the curriculum.

JOE R. BURNETT is professor of philosophy of education and acting dean, College of Education, University of Illinois, Champaign-Urbana. He is a past president of the Philosophy of Education Society and a member of the Advisory Board of the Center for Dewey Studies, Southern Illinois University, Carbondale.

THOMAS F. GREEN is professor of education, Syracuse University. His interests focus upon philosophy of education, social theory, and public policy. His forthcoming book is *On the Behavior of Educational Systems*, to be published by Syracuse University Press, Spring 1980.

RICHARD PRATTE is professor of education at The Ohio State University, where he teaches the philosophy of education. He received his doctorate from the University of Connecticut, Storrs, and previously taught at the University of Bridgeport and the University of Akron. He is the author of *The Public School Movement, Ideology and Education, Contemporary Theories of Education*, and numerous articles and essays in such journals as *Intellect, The Educational Forum, Educational Theory*, and *The Journal of General Education*.

JONAS F. SOLTIS is William Heard Kilpatrick Professor in philosophy and education at Teachers College, Columbia University, and is a past president of the Philosophy of Education Society. He is serving as editor for the forthcoming NSSE yearbook on philosophy of education to be published in 1981. Among his numerous articles and books are: "Analysis and Anomalies in Philosophy of Education," *Seeing, Knowing, and Believing*, and the recent second edition of *An Introduction to the Analysis of Educational Concepts*, which extends his work on the pedagogy of analytic skills development.

DONALD VANDENBERG is reader in education at Queensland University, Australia. He formerly taught at Calgary, Pennsylvania State, and the University of California at Los Angeles. His major research interest in the past decade has been the ethical foundations of education.

Preface

The projected 1981 publication of a National Society for the Study of Education (NSSE) yearbook on philosophy of education provided the impetus for commissioning a special issue of the *Teachers College Record* that appeared in early 1980 (vol. 81, no. 2, winter 1979). This book is a reprint of that special issue.

In the course of developing the format and content of the yearbook, it became apparent to the editorial committee that while it would be highly desirable, it would not be possible to treat the recent history of philosophy of education adequately and also provide the yearbook's readers with a broad representative sample of contemporary work in the field. Therefore, the decision was made to seek another vehicle for displaying the developments in philosophy of education since mid-century that might serve as a prefatory and companion volume to the yearbook. Douglas Sloan, historian and editor of the *Teachers College Record,* generously offered one issue of the *Record* for that purpose and Teachers College Press has sponsored this subsequent publication. The remainder of this Preface is drawn from my descriptive introductory remarks to that special issue of the *Record,* which were designed to orient the reader to the essays that follow. I trust that they will serve the same purpose here.

While highlighting some of the major developments in philosophy of education since mid-century and treating such central topics as analytic and linguistic philosophy, existentialism and phenomenology, and educational policy studies, this special issue is not intended to be a rigorous historical record of scholarship in the field from 1950 to 1980. In fact, with the general reader in mind, much of the technical work and scholarly debate of the last thirty years in philosophy of education has been left out and even some major philosophical positions and works slighted in an attempt to display the field in broad strokes. The general reader will also miss what might be called ideological, romantic, utopian, critical, and policy-oriented popular philosophical reflections on education that were put forward by serious educational thinkers during this same period and ranged from critical descriptions of educational "wastelands," "mindlessness," and inhumanity toward children to designs for "educating the public" and proposals to "deschool" society. Their omission is not a negative appraisal of their worth, but it is to mark an important difference between two very useful and compatible meanings of philosophy of education in its "public" and "professional" senses.

In its broad and basic *public* sense, having a philosophy of education is quite similar to having a philosophy of life and being philosophical in this sense is being deeply concerned and thoughtfully reflective about fundamental aspects of educating in our time. This sense connotes the important and abiding concern of educators, statesmen, journalists, intellectuals, citizens, *and* philosophers with the purposes, root problems, social policies, and new visions of educating. This is not the singular province of those professionals trained in philosophy of education nor should it be. Education is such a central and crucial social and cultural institution that the thoughtful design and appraisal of it should be and is open to any who would aspire to provide thoughtful leadership for our society and its schools.

But there is also a narrower, more technical, and *professional* sense of philosophy of education. In this century, for the first time in the history of education, philosophers have been trained singularly and directly in the field of philosophy of education, developed a scholarly literature of their own, and brought technical philosophical perspective to bear on educational theory, policy, and practice. Just as we do not expect every historian to rewrite the history of civilization nor every psychologist to be the next Freud, so it would be unrealistic to expect each and every philosopher of education to invent a new philosophy of education, to provide the definitive critique of contemporary educational practice, and to set once and for all our national educational goals. As professional educators we appreciate the scholarly work of historians, psychologists, sociologists, and other such scholars precisely to the degree that they help us see, understand, and make better sense of some aspect of what we are doing. So too ought it to be with the professional educational philosophers who bring their technical training and skills to bear on relevant educational-philosophical matters.

Each of the articles in this special issue in its own way will show that over the last thirty years philosophy of education in the professional sense has become more technically philosophical and has been aimed primarily at helping educators see more clearly some aspect of what they are about from the technical perspective of philosophy. The practicing philosophical scholar in education has tried to stimulate thought, elucidate meaning, provide critical appraisals, force careful judgment, and create conceptual frameworks for understanding the many philosophical dimensions of the complex business of education in our highly specialized world.

One of the major problems blocking the more effective use of this scholarly philosophical work in education has been the mismatch between the educator's expectations and the philosopher's contributions. If one looks to philosophy of education expecting to find philosophy only in the public sense and sees a narrower professional offering, no matter what its potential value, there can be disappointment and lack of appreciation. Obviously, *both* public and professional contributions in philosophy of education are important, needed, and valuable. This special issue has been designed to repair this mismatch of expectations between the two by providing the general reader with a sense of what professional philosophers of education recently have been about and what to expect from them in the near future.

—Jonas F. Soltis
New York, N.Y.
December 1980

Philosophy of Education
since Mid-Century

Philosophy of Education between Yearbooks

HARRY S. BROUDY
University of Illinois, Urbana

Opinions differ as to whether education is a craft, a profession, an institution, or just another name for the proper nurture of the young. However, if it is to be regarded as a profession coordinate with other professions, it shares two tasks with them. One is to find a theory (*logos*) that explains its procedures (*techné*). The other is to formulate a "philosophy of" that explicates and justifies its claim on society for prestige and remuneration. Assuming optimistically that sciencelike disciplines will provide the makings of a theory, where is a profession such as education to find its philosophy? Clearly from philosophy. But what if philosophy is too remote from the particulars of professional practice?

A volume published in 1945 entitled *Philosophy in American Education* replied:

> If the philosopher will accept the responsibility of making his ideas fit the particular subject matter in which the specialist is working, and if the specialist in his turn is willing to think through his own assumptions to the point at which their philosophical meaning can be clearly stated and responsibly judged, they will jointly have something to say in the interpretation of their common subject that will be worth hearing and worth teaching.[1]

In 1942, the forty-first yearbook of the National Society for the Study of Education (NSSE), Part I, entitled *Philosophies of Education*, had already anticipated this question, and a second yearbook, called *Modern Philosophies and Education* (1955), carried it further. On the eve of the preparation of a third yearbook, the details of which are discussed by Professor Jonas F. Soltis in his article in this issue, it may be helpful to review the content and style of the first two. The articles in this issue are concerned with developments in the field that will shape the new volume.

This article is a version of the introductory chapter that Harry S. Broudy prepared for the eightieth NSSE yearbook and appears here with the permission of the NSSE Board of Directors.

Philosophy of education did not wait until 1942 to be born, but in the teacher education curricula, courses bearing that name were not uniformly related to formal philosophy. A philosophy of education referred to a set of beliefs about life and schooling. Sometimes these beliefs were the results of "being thoughtful or reflective about education." Often they embodied proverbial wisdom about the young or long experience in the schools. School personnel were expected to have a set of beliefs of this kind, and candidates for teaching and administrative positions were often asked: "What is your philosophy of education?"

However, formal philosophies of education, those of Plato, Comenius, Froebel, Herbart, Rousseau, for example, often found their way into philosophy of education courses. The yearbooks noted above made a conscious effort to relate very general ideas about life and schooling to types of philosophical thought. Since 1955, philosophy of education has acquired new modes of inquiry, constituencies, and tasks; it is now expected to be more than a set of general beliefs about schooling or a way of classifying such beliefs according to philosophical typology.

Readers of the first two NSSE yearbooks on the philosophy of education will be struck by the differences in their rationales. In justifying the 1942 volume, John Brubacher cited the need for philosophy in "the muddled times in which we live." They were indeed muddled, trailing the Great Depression and ushering in American participation in World War II, although the book says very little about either.

As for the muddled times in education, Brubacher mentions the impact of science and industrialism on the schools and the questioning of "a long-accepted political idea of education" as contributing to the confusion about the aims of schooling (p. 3). Hence the desire for an inclusive theory of education presumably to dispel the confusion. Brubacher notes that a number of such theories (philosophies) had been developed, but that often educators were acquainted with only one of them. A yearbook setting forth a variety of theories would correct this "professional astigmatism" (p. 4).

The variety included a historical overview by Edward H. Reisner titled "Philosophy and Science in the Western World"; Experimentalism by William H. Kilpatrick; Realism by Frederick S. Breed; Idealism by Herman H. Horne; Catholicism by William J. McGucken. These were followed by a defense of philosophy of education by Mortimer J. Adler and a chapter by Brubacher comparing the views of the diverse philosophical positions on traits of reality, knowledge, human nature and learning, educational values, school and society, and conflict, communication, and cooperation. Brubacher thus identified themes to which a philosophy did or should address itself. How much consensus this identification represented is hard to say, because he reports that the committee could not agree on larger problems, "not even . . . as to what constitutes a problem in the philosophy of education" (p. 5).

In his opening chapter of the fifty-fourth yearbook, Brubacher attributed the great interest in educational philosophy to the challenge of Progressive education. It was, as he noted, a challenge not only to traditional schooling patterns but also to the accepted social and philosophical rationales for education. The strife of educational ideologies interrupted by World War II was resumed at its close. The Philosophy of Education Society had been revived, and its annual meetings in the decade after 1945 were animated by the debates between the advocates and foes of the philosophies that had been articulated in the forty-first yearbook and some views not there represented.[2]

The main motivations of the fifty-fourth yearbook, according to Brubacher, were (1) anxiety that modern education was adrift, (2) that current aims of education were either vague or conflicting and did not generate strong loyalty, (3) anxiety over "serious letdown in standards of instruction as a result of modern educational procedures," (4) lack of confidence in a democratic conception of education, (5) concern that schools allow children too much freedom, and (6) that schools are neglecting religion (pp. 15–16).

Neither yearbook committee seemed to doubt philosophy's potential for dealing with muddles and relieving anxieties. Despite increased diversity in philosophical theorizing, the 1955 committee still believed that the best way to get an overall view of the problems of men and education was to examine them through the stencil or lens of a philosophical system or school or ism.

The fifty-fourth yearbook embodied several significant changes, however. First, it entrusted the writing of the chapters to "real" philosophers, but provided each with a philosopher of education to keep him relevant, so to speak, to problems of education. In the second place, the inability of the committee of the forty-first yearbook to define the problems of philosophy of education presumably had been overcome, and the writers were instructed to include sections dealing with (1) a general philosophical orientation; (2) aims, values, and curriculum; (3) the educative process, its methods, motivation, and the like; (4) school and society; (5) the school and the individual; and (6) religious and moral education.

The third difference was in some of the positions chosen for representation. Realism was represented by John Wild; Thomism by Jacques Maritain; Idealism by Theodore M. Greene, who wrote "A Liberal Christian Idealist Philosophy of Education"; Experimentalism was represented by George R. Geiger; Marxism by Robert S. Cohen; Existentialism by Ralph Harper; the linguistic approach (to be distinguished from ordinary language analysis) by Kenneth Burke; logical empiricism by Herbert Feigl; and a chapter called "Ontological Philosophy of Education" by James K. Feibleman.

The decision to have chapters written by philosophers rather than by philosophers of education reflects an awareness on the part of some of the prominent figures in the Philosophy of Education Society that philosophy of education needed more philosophy. This, in turn, was the result of studies (including one by R. Bruce Raup of Teachers College, Columbia) and general observation that philosophy of education courses were often taught by instructors relatively innocent of training in formal philosophy.[3]

The 1942 and 1954 yearbooks reflected the view that philosophy of education should be a field of scholarly inquiry, writing, and teaching. It was more than being thoughtful about education and more than the proverbial wisdom about schooling. It was different from—if not more than—the history of educational institutions. It was also different from psychology and sociology of education. The differences were marked by the word "philosophy." Some knowledge of what is included in the college catalog under that rubric was thought to be essential to philosophy of education. It was to be expected that this trend in educational philosophy would reflect developments in general philosophy. What, then, was the situation in that field in the forties?

In 1945 the Commission on the Function of Philosophy in American Education published a report to its parent, the American Philosophical Association.[4] The original proposal for the report was made in 1943 and as part of its inquiry the commission interviewed educators, public figures, and philosophers, including some philosophers of education. The volume, therefore, is a valuable statement of how general philosophy was being perceived at that time by philosophers and philosophers of education. And it came at the time when philosophy of education was experiencing a new, postwar impetus.

Blanshard summarized the "reproaches" to philosophy (mostly from within the ranks of philosophers) as follows:

First, it was ensconced in an ivory tower, busy with such "trifles" as sense data, the meaning of meaning, reduction of the number of primitive propositions required by deductive logic, and whether all or some a priori statements are tautologous.

Furthermore, where was philosophy in times of crisis? For example, the "three most prominent schools of ethical thought hold respectively that the moral philosophy of the past 'rests on a mistake,' that moral standards are group customs with no validity beyond the group, and that moral judgments have no significance at all."[5]

The critics charged that there was no agreement on what philosophy says; that philosophers were negative "artists of demolition of belief"; that philosophy's knowledge was imperfect—it could not unite the disciplines nor achieve competence in them. Finally, philosophers were crabbed in expression, needlessly technical, unlike Mill and William James, who could talk to plain men.

It is natural enough that young writers who feel uncertain of themselves should stud their text with technicalities; they want the record to show that they know the tools of their trade; and if it does show that, they are content to forget for the time that a "platitude is not turned into a profundity by being dressed up as a conundrum." But when this and worse are done by veteran philosophers, supposed in virtue of their profession to be connoisseurs of clear and orderly exposition, readers are not likely to be tolerant.[6]

These criticisms of philosophy were not new. They rejected the high expectations nurtured by speculative idealism, which dominated the closing years of the nineteenth century, during which philosophy in America first won wide recognition as an autonomous field of study. It was the time of Howison, Royce, Creighton, Wenley, and their associates. The philosopher was the "judge and critic of both science and theology . . . based on speculative insight into the nature of ultimate reality."[7]

Murphy remarked that

their [the Absolute Idealists] warrant to speak for Absolute Reality . . . has been called in question. But in presenting to their confused contemporaries the ideal of rational wholeness and of comprehensive justice to all aspects of experience . . . : they performed an essential philosophical function.[8]

It is important to note that the Pragmatism of James and Dewey had already challenged speculative Idealism, and that by the time the book was published various types of Realism and Naturalism had been challenging both Idealism and Pragmatism. It was an age of isms, and a thinker could take his or her choice of them.

In the late twenties and most of the thirties, the commission noted, the college student was introduced to philosophy by a study of types or isms in which the instructor maintained a more or less neutral stance. It was this pattern that was adopted by both yearbooks. However, the relation of the yearbooks to the content and modes of inquiry in general philosophy is harder to match up on the basis of the commission report. For example, Murphy notes that in the forties, philosophy had already witnessed a strong interest in formal or symbolic logic. Logic was to be studied as a discipline, but also as a tool to get rid of many "pseudo" problems in metaphysics. He adds, however, that:

> Meanwhile the battle of the positivists and the metaphysicians has bred a suspicion of symbolic logic in the traditionalist camp and a contempt of historical philosophy among the analysts. . . .[9]

One does not get a strong impression of these developments in the forty-first yearbook, and if I am not mistaken, even the fifty-fourth volume does not reflect the extent to which general philosophy had become devoted to the logical purification of philosophical discourse, despite the inclusion of Feigl's chapter on logical empiricism. On the other hand, it is a bit surprising that the commission report published in 1945 did not include in its index the names of Wittgenstein, Kierkegaard, Husserl, and Heidegger—possibly because they had not yet become established in the general introductory courses in philosophy.

One is hard put to decide whether Murphy was premature or prescient in his estimate of the effect of the strong critical emphasis in philosophy. He concluded that "this dialectical achievement has failed, so far at least, to eventuate in any corresponding philosophical wisdom or to make effective connection with the public mind."[10]

He continues:

> Nor is the reason for all this at all hard to find. Most men who turn to philosophy for guidance [and surely educators must be included here] want not arguments but conclusions: they are concerned not so much to avoid error as to arrive at truth. . . . What seems to be established is that the major philosophies so far devised have involved grave lapses in logical or linguistic propriety, and that while, properly translated into an analytically purified language, they might possiby be true, there is no good reason to suppose that in any case they are. The better we understand logic, Bertrand Russell has characteristically remarked, the less we find that we can prove

and the more, consequently, that we must accept on nonlogical grounds, if we are not to land in a rationally immaculate but unlivable skepticism.[11]

It would take a careful historical study to establish the precise synchrony between the views entertained by general philosophers and philosophers of education and perhaps it is not too important to do so. More important is that as philosophy of education shifted more of its attention to the logical and linguistic analysis of educational concepts and problems, it shifted away from the isms approach. The shift was most rapid in colleges of education located in research-oriented universities that concentrated on advanced graduate study, somewhat less rapid in schools devoting their major efforts to undergraduate teacher preparation, and much less in the minds and discourse of school personnel who learned their philosophy of education from texts that used the isms format.

Aside from the circumstance that courses in philosophy frequently had been organized in this way in college departments, there was a belief that each philosophical system as it formulated an epistemology, metaphysics, and ethics would ground beliefs about the real, the true, and the good. Hence the notion that an ism or a well-worked-out system of philosophy would yield a rational guidance to life and education seemed obvious. Increasingly, departments of philosophy are offering courses in such subareas as philosophy of science, philosophy of language, philosophy of politics, and so forth. The layman, one can be sure, will continue to identify philosophy with a search for and love of wisdom, even though college catalogs almost never include wisdom among offerings of departments of philosophy.[12] Likewise, the layman will continue to look to a philosophy of education for more than logical purity and wholesome skepticism. People are not and do not want schools to be neutral about the life they want for their children as citizens, workers, and persons.

Whether there is a logical warrant for finding guidance and norms in systems of philosophy is another matter. During the fifties there was much heated debate among philosophers of education as to whether a value "ought" could be deduced from a factual "is," and whether from a theory about the good in general, prescriptions for educational practice could be determined.[13] In general, the tide of philosophical argument and sentiment was negative. The positivists were pushing the fact-value distinction for all that it was or was not worth, depriving assertions of value of all empirical truth claims—and no others were regarded by them as legitimate. Doubt was expressed that the nature of man could be arrived at rationally by any system of inquiry or definition, and that even if the *telos*, the natural end of man, could be discovered, it would still leave open the question as to whether it was good. But all of this took place in the academy and had relatively little effect on the educational practitioner's convictions that some forms of conduct were more consonant with the ideals of humanity than others. The layman is incurably metaphysical, and if the philosophy of education ignores or merely makes fun of this need, it will be satisfied by nonphilosophical sources.

Four lines of philosophical thinking that have been prominent in the literature of the last two decades are discussed in the articles by Richard Pratte, Donald Vandenberg, Joe R. Burnett, and Thomas Green. Pratte deals with the development of analysis, Vandenberg with Existentialism and Phenomenology, while Burnett describes the continuity and one might say "renewed" interest in the writings of John Dewey and Green treats the role of philosophy in educational policy studies. However, we also may have entered and gone some way into a period in which both general and educational philosophy have turned more of their attention to substantive questions that have always engaged systematic philosophies. These problems are the current versions of the perennial conflict between freedom and necessity, individuality and the common good, personhood and mass society, justice and compassion, mores and morals, mass and class, truth and credibility. The concern with social justice, the environment, peace, the third world, and many other agitations of the late sixties and the early seventies have given impetus to neo-Marxism, a variety of existentialism, cultism, and even occultism in academia, not excluding the departments of philosophy and philosophy of education. Humanism and the problems of humanity that students discussed in courses organized according to isms are once more in the forefront of scholarly attention, albeit the new and the old humanisms do not always sound like variations on the same theme.

It may be of some significance that twenty-five years will have elapsed between the last yearbook on the philosophy of education and the current one. Only thirteen years separated the first two. Surely it does not signify a lack of writing in the field that needed summarizing. On the contrary, an examination of the *Proceedings* of the Philosophy of Education Society, *Educational Theory, Studies in Philosophy and Education*, text materials, and so forth, reveals a high volume of work in the fifties and early sixties.

A more plausible conjecture is that between 1955 and 1970, the years when another yearbook might have been expected, both the styles of doing philosophy of education and the problems facing philosophers of education had changed too radically to permit a definitive summarization.

The length of the interval may also be a result of problems created by the new relationships between school administrators, teachers, teacher preparation institutions, and the bureaucratic workers in the Department of Health, Education, and Welfare, the National Institute of Education, and half a hundred other federal and state agencies that funded, regulated, or monitored schools after the mid-sixties. In 1965, civil rights legislation marked a watershed in schooling at all levels. There followed a great upheaval on campuses about matters that touched fundamental issues in truth and value, and the relation of school to society. The Vietnam War was only one of the causes of the upheaval, but one of its aftermaths—more enduring than the protest activism itself—was the liberation or emancipation of individuals from legal and moral restrictions that characterized the middle-class American establishment. This is an enduring aftermath because so many of the middle class have adopted or co-opted the right to self-gratification, to do their own thing and to live "their own lives." Even the current public reaction against those some have called the underclass in our society (the chronically poor) does not always signify a return to the austere work ethic attributed to the Protestants. On the contrary, all classes define political and moral justice as the right to consume more and more. Some have called this mood materialism, others have dubbed it the new hedonism (the desire to be thin but rich). The loss of credibility suffered by virtually all professions and institutions also is grounded in the belief that private interest, greed for money, power, and privilege, are the "true" motives of persons in power, and that the beginning of wisdom is not to believe what one hears or reads to the contrary. The rage for litigation now open to dissidents, oppositionists, and hitherto helpless victims is greeted gleefully by those who see the mighty hoist by their own petard, the courts, and, with no less glee, the hordes of lawyers for whom it is an ill wind indeed that does not blow up a new class of clients.

It would be strange indeed if the schools were not affected by these changes and that schools would not reflect the ambiguities of parents and citizens toward their children, their spouses, their new life-styles.

The rapid (about five-year intervals) shift from a curriculum devoted to excellence in academic subjects to one that concentrated on compassion for and understanding of the newly enfranchised minorities and thence to a return to basics were symptoms of shifts in social ideology. The accountability movements and the efforts of the federal government to implement civil and human rights legislation were matters of morality as well as economics and law. The rapidly changing life-styles revived once more the cries for moral education, which were also cries for help from philosophers. In answering these cries, or at least in discussing them, philosophers of education were splashed by more existential mud than they might have wished.

Philosophers of education did much to clarify the intuition that there is a difference between action and behavior, education and training, behavior modification and teaching. In the sixties, philosophers of education played an important part in bringing to public awareness the import of certain school practices for the rights of persons and the meaning of a humane society. They were in the forefront of the discussion on the role of the school in the industrial and postindustrial society. Some philosophers of education were themselves activists; others reflected on activism, radicalism, anarchism, libertarianism, and their opposites.

The more specialized interests and activities of philosophers of education are also reflected in the NSSE decision to issue a yearbook on the philosophical redirection of educational research (1972) and the American Educational Research Association's decision to include in its series of research a volume on the philosophy of educational research.[14]

There is little doubt that the departure from the isms approach will disturb many educators who were introduced to the philosophy of education and perhaps to philosophy itself through introductory courses of this kind. At least one important professional group is currently spending considerable time and money classifying its own goals, policies, organization, and procedures according to five isms. Logical niceties about the validity of the approach do not weaken their conviction that each of the five philosophies is a distinctive way of looking at knowledge, reality, and value, and that seeing education through these lenses will reveal something important about their own field.

Today philosophy of education, Janus-like, is facing two ways at once. It speaks to philosophers of education, that is, the academic guild whose members teach courses in the field to prospective teachers and doctoral students, but it also speaks to educators at all levels of schooling. It is concerned with problems of philosophy, on the one hand, and problems of schooling, on the other. This duality of audiences and tasks engenders differences in language, interests, and channels of communication.

The language in which philosophers of education write and speak to each other and to their graduate students is more technical and abstract than their discourse with public school teachers and administrators. When talking to each other, their attention tends to veer toward the logical aspects of argument and the conceptualization of problems. Yet to teachers and school administrators, the pragmatic aspects of goals, curriculum, organization, and teaching-learning are primary, not the niceties of argument, and the discourse must demand a minimum of technical and esoteric sophistication.

Presumably, the primary audience and the focal problems of philosophy of education remain educational, but the tensions between obligations to practitioners and to the field as a domain for academic inquiry were heightened as the study of philosophy of education in the fifties and sixties became more philosophical and increasingly a field for doctoral specialization.

Philosophers of education communicate with their diverse constituencies through different channels. They reach educational personnel in courses that are preservice or in-service components of baccalaureate and graduate programs. There was a time when virtually all "professional" programs *required* some study in the foundations, including philosophical foundations. During the campus turmoils of the sixties, foundations courses often provided platforms for promulgating the spirit of counterculture. This spirit was not conducive to stability of course content or structure. As a result, some embarrassing questions were asked about the justification of courses without stipulated distinctive content being "required" on the ground that they were too important for any prospective educators to miss. Nevertheless, the flood of college students in the sixties kept enrollments in schools of education and in foundations courses comfortably high. It also promised and provided jobs for doctoral students to teach these courses.

Outside of formal courses, school people learn what the philosopher of education has to say through articles that occasionally appear in the professional journals to which they subscribe. There is little reason to believe that many of them subscribe to or read journals devoted to the philosophy of education. Occasionally, philosophers of education may be heard at conferences attended by administrators, college teachers of education, and classroom teachers. As philosophy of education faculties move into policy studies, they may be heard from more frequently both in journals and at conferences outside of their own field of specialization. However, in the great societal and educational controversies of the last decade, neither philosophers nor philosophers of education were consulted in high places nor did their views command much attention in the educational establishment. Thomas Green, in his article in this issue, speaks to the role of philosophy in educational policymaking.

Philosophers of education communicate with each other through the meetings and proceedings of a national organization, the Philosophy of Education Society; regional groups; and journals devoted to studies in the field. With the parent discipline of philosophy, philosophy of education communicates through the doctoral program. For as doctoral programs increased in number and popularity, a greater proportion of the requirements for the degree were allocated to courses in the philosophy department and philosophers were often asked to serve as members of doctoral committees. This had a dual effect. First, it attracted bright young people with an aptitude for the kind of abstract thinking required for the study of philosophy. For some of these, as might be expected, the messy problems of education, which are supposed to be the texts of the philosophy of education, became the pretexts for doing general philosophy, especially in their dissertations and contributions to their professional publications.

The other effect of the greater ingestion of philosophy by doctoral students was the widespread adoption of the analytical modes (linguistic and logical) of philosophizing by philosophers of education. In time, the doctoral students became professors, and admirable though their desire for logical clarity and linguistic honesty was, the putative patients of their therapeutic analysis did not always discern the relevance of the cure to their disease. It became more difficult for philosophers of education to communicate with educators.

The diversity of audiences, problems, and channels of communication raises the question as to which audiences and at what level a yearbook should be aimed. How far down the abstract-concrete scale can a yearbook in the philosophy of education go and still remain philosophical? How far up can it go without losing touch with nonphilosophical audiences?

These questions are especially important now because with the shrinking of public school enrollments and a corresponding reduction in the demand for teachers, the market for teachers of the philosophy of education has been depressed for several years. Furthermore, various accountability movements fertilized competency-based programs of teacher preparation and prompted demands for more field experience and less theoretical course work. In one state the accreditation officials said that foundations could qualify as requirements if they could be stated as behavioral objectives. Translating philosophical processes into behaviorally defined "competences" has not always been a rewarding enterprise and by some has been called "mindless" in both the literal and figurative senses of the term.

WHAT HAVE EDUCATORS A RIGHT TO EXPECT FROM PHILOSOPHY OF EDUCATION?

1. They have a right to expect that philosophers of education will address themselves to problems of education in general and as those problems impinge on schooling. Problems arising in the formulation of aims, curriculum, organization, teaching-learning, and research methodology qualify as educational problems. Not all educational problems are philosophical, however. Some are technical; some economic; some are administrational; some have to do with matters of fact; some appeal to theories of empirical science. It is only when an educational problem requires the concepts of logic, epistemology, metaphysics, ethics, or aesthetics that philosophy becomes relevant. Indeed, one of the more useful services philosophers of education can render is to clarify the bounds of this relevance and to point out just what sort of evidence is relevant. In this connection the educator has a related right not to be expected to cope with technical problems in philosophy or educational problems couched in highly technical philosophical language.

Yet there is a limit to what the philosopher can do by way of translation for school people who have not had some work in the philosophy of education and preferably in general philosophy as well. This is why courses in philosophy of education should be part of the professional preparation of all education personnel and some work in general philosophy should be required as a preprofessional prerequisite.

2. Educators have a right to expect from philosophers of education a clarification and elucidation of concepts and arguments used in educational literature, especially in the literature of educational controversy. Voucher systems, minimum competency testing, equality of educational opportunity, integration, are examples of such issues. The educator can expect from the philosopher of education (a) reasoned proposals to use terms in one way rather than another so that ambiguity, equivocation, and vagueness can be eliminated; (b) reasoned proposals that a controversy be adjudicated in one way rather

than another. What school people cannot expect is consensus on usage or judgment from the philosophers. (Aside from the fact that philosophers are not likely to agree on philosophical issues, issues cease to be philosophical when such agreement is reached—at least they cease to be of philosophical interest once they are settled.)

3. School people have a right to expect from the philosopher of education a careful examination of proposals and policies with respect to their consequences and possibilities, in the round, so to speak. This the philosopher of education does by examining issues in a variety of contexts: social, moral, ideological. For example, the moral dimension of the Bakke decision is properly a philosophical problem, but it is also the business of the philosophy of education to explicate its political and educational consequences as well.[15]

4. Educators also have the right to expect from at least some writers in the philosophy of education a synoptic, systematic, coherent set of beliefs and arguments about education that deals with the educational enterprise as a whole and that makes connection with a philosophy of life.

5. Finally, educators have a right to expect from philosophy of education a strong and steady advocacy of rational discussion, freedom of inquiry, and instead of a fixed faith "an interest and standard from which reliable beliefs can spring."[16]

One cannot expect everyone writing in the field to fulfill all of these expectations. There is bound to be a diversity of interest with a corresponding variety of literatures from which courses in the philosophy of education will be composed. But it is fair to expect that good courses in philosophy of education will introduce students to the philosophical aspects of the major issues in education.

Footnotes

1 Brand Blanshard et al., *Philosophy in American Education* (New York: Harper & Brothers, 1945), p. 234.

2 And animated they were. Before concurrent paper sessions were instituted, most of the annual meeting was devoted to plenary sessions at which various positions were interpreted, defended against misinterpretation and attack, and praised as incorporating the virtues claimed by the other views, but not their vices. Until the late fifties, the pivot on which most discussions revolved was John Dewey. What he said, what he meant, what he should have said, and, of course, whether it was true, were rarely absent from the argument on the floor or in the corridors. The Ohio State version of the Dewey doctrine was represented by Henry "Hank" Hullfish and Ernest (Ernie) Bayles. The latter was especially sensitive to the slightest odor of absolutes. He opposed them ably, vigorously, and absolutely not only against Thomists and Realists, but against backsliding Pragmatists as well.

3   Beginning in the middle forties, Brubacher, Kenneth Benne, George Axtelle, Louise Antz, R. Bruce Raup, and Theodore Brameld were especially active in trying to promote more scholarly work in the field. I am sure there were others, but this group met with some regularity in New York and was more familiar to me. Brubacher and Robert Ulich were especially influential in organizing the New England region of the Philosophy of Education Society.

4   Blanshard et al., *Philosophy in American Education.*

5   Ibid., p. 32.

6   Ibid., p. 38.

7   Arthur E. Murphy in ibid., p. 43.

8   Ibid., p. 47.

9   Ibid., p. 57.

10   Ibid., p. 55.

11   Ibid.

12   Wisdom, as the late Oliver Martin observed, is studied in the English department and language in the philosophy department.

13   *Harvard Educational Review* 2, no. 26 (1956) and 4, no. 28 (Fall 1958); and *Journal of Philosophy* 2, no. 52 (1955).

14   Harry S. Broudy, Robert H. Ennis, and Leonard I. Krimmerman, eds., *Philosophy of Educational Research* (New York: John Wiley, 1973).

15   Allan Bakke was denied admission to the University of California at Davis Medical School. The U.S. Supreme Court upheld Bakke's contention that a quota system kept him out in favor of minority candidates with lower admissions scores.

16   Blanshard et al., *Philosophy in American Education*, p. 108.

Analytic Philosophy of Education:
A Historical Perspective

RICHARD PRATTE
Ohio State University

INTRODUCTION

When one utters the word philosophy outside of philosophical circles, people think of a wide variety of things. Many, I am sure, think first and foremost of general ideas, especially in their relation to social and political affairs. For example, it is not considered quite remarkable for someone outside of academe to know the "social" philosophers such as John Dewey, Karl Marx, Frederick Nietzsche, and Jean-Paul Sartre. Others, more generally, consider philosophy to be the logical clarification of thought. Still others may think about logic and language and how these have come to be identified with philosophy today.

When one utters the word philosophy within philosophical circles one is likely to be confronted with the recognition that there is a great divide in the history of philosophy. Philosophy appears to be a two-headed hydra going in opposite directions. One branch has maintained a close affinity with the affairs of the heart and seeks the best possible interpretation of the world as we know it. This branch includes the existentialists, social philosophers, and phenomenologists. Most of the popular, even faddist, philosophers of the past 100 years have come from this branch, which maintains that the only knowledge worth having is knowledge that bears directly on the human experience.

The other branch of philosophy has a less grand aim. It restricts the scope of philosophy to coincide with the limits of reason and tends toward logic and language, thus intensifing philosophy's concern with argument and the structure and precision of language meaning. This is the branch of analytic philosophy that focuses on the tools of inquiry more intensely than on its objects, tending to relegate to the meaningless that which cannot be rigorously proved.

Prior to the publication of the 1955 National Society for the Study of Education (NSSE) yearbook,[1] the study of philosophy of education ignored the fact that analytic philosophy had come to dominate Western philosophy, first in England and later in the United States. Indeed, many American philosophers came to stand in the forefront of this movement. But it was not until the late 1950s that the beam of analytic philosophy of education (hereafter "analysis") was lit in the United States, appearing first as a small unwanted child to the older traditional view of philosophy of education.

The traditional view of philosophy of education was that of educationists engaging in speculation concerning philosophical issues in education. It was the heir of the philosophic tradition that took the affairs of the heart quite seriously, attempting to give the best possible interpretation of the world *and* its application in terms of "implication" for educational policy and practice.[2]

This is not to say that a survey of articles in philosophy of education, or even a comprehensive survey of the origins of all philosophic positions, would find a lack of rigorous attention to language, its meaning and structure. For example, one cannot for a moment doubt that Plato illustrated a system-building approach to philosophy, but it cannot equally be denied that he ignored analytic method, for he was concerned with an explicit and practicable method of philosophic analysis. In other words, clarification of language goes back to philosophy's beginnings; it has always been there. What is new in contemporary analytic philosophy is the emphasis given to language analysis as methodology as well as the linguistic and logical tools polished to a high degree.

The traditional branch of philosophy of education commonly divided into "schools" or "isms." Now there is no doubt that the division of philosophies into schools is always a somewhat artificial matter, since every philosopher worthy of the name will say what he or she thinks whether it agrees with the thought of a colleague or not. But before the advent of analysis a large number of educational philosophers accepted certain labels—Pragmatist, Idealist, Realist, and so on—even though they have preferred another variant of it. They held in common as basic tenets a particular view of metaphysics, humankind, and of the Good Life, and how these somehow formed the basis of the unity of educational theory and practice.

Although this view dominated educational philosophy, three related problems in particular were especially critical. First, many of the educationists lacked an adequate training in philosophy, regardless of how that might be defined. Perhaps an analogy with clinical psychology might be helpful in explaining this phenomenon. In clinical psychology we have the example of Sigmund Freud, who was trained as a physician and considered an M.D. essential to practicing clinical psychology. Later, others rejected this model and produced

clinical psychologists rather than psychiatrists. Analogously, we see Boyd H. Bode (Ohio State University, 1921–1944) coming into philosophy of education from academic philosophy. Bode and his contemporaries founded the study of philosophy of education and contributed widely to its body of knowledge. Other philosophers, such as John Dewey, Alfred North Whitehead, and Bertrand Russell, made contributions to educational philosophy but maintained the study of philosophy to be their life's work.

Bode's students, however, were not trained as academic philosophers but as philosophers of education. After a generation or so of producing educational philosophers, course work in philosophy was not considered essential in the philosophy of education program at Ohio State University. Henry "Hank" Hullfish, a student and successor of Bode, regarded course work in philosophy, at least in the philosophy department at Ohio State University, as antithetical to the development of a knowledgeable pragmatic educational philosopher.[3]

Thus the development of educationist philosophers of education parallels the development of clinical psychologists. Educational philosophers were not trained in departments of philosophy in ethics, epistemology, or aesthetics, using educational situations or issues as a context for investigation, but were trained in colleges of education to deal with the practical problems of classroom procedures and practices.

The second problem arose due to the fact of unprecedented schooling expansion. As public schooling expanded in the 1950s and 1960s, there was created a great demand for teachers and the expansion of teacher education. Concomitantly, a demand was created for teachers of educational philosophy, a fact not unnoticed by colleges of education. Hence, educationists produced educationists to fill the void and in the process the intimate relation between academic philosophy and philosophy of education, already strained, was ruptured—so much so that a cult phenomenon developed in educational philosophy that reveled in the fact that educational philosophy was something other than academic philosophy, somehow more "real" and "practical."

Finally, the separation of academic philosophy from educational philosophy was made secure by the professional movement in education. To be an educational philosopher one had to be concerned with professional matters, usually interpreted as educational problems or issues studied from the vantage point of such matters as "discipline," "motivation," "school finance," "innovation," and so on. In order to be relevant in the classroom, educational philosophers sought respectability with other educationists by eschewing traditional philosophic issues in favor of social or cultural approaches. Hence, one segment of educational philosophy turned from the traditional "isms" to the alleged more relevant "isms" of progressivism, essentialism, perennialism, and reconstructionism, teasing out of these their "implications" for practical educational problems.[4]

Thus in the 1950s the function of philosophy of education in teacher education programs was either to provide students with a directive for life and its connection to the schoolroom or to be relevant to the problems or issues of everyday classroom teaching. The former approach gave students "something to believe in or die for," the latter was a problem-oriented approach to teaching. In either case, however, students were not likely to learn much of philosophy, especially linguistic or logical methodology.

With this as the background, it might be said that analysis developed, at least in part, as a reaction to a mode of philosophy of education that denied the importance of methodology. Students commonly studied and learned the product of another's thought and missed philosophy of education as an activity, a doing. It is thus that analysis gave a completely different direction to the study of philosophy of education. The direction is, at least in part, away from a prescriptive or systems approach, with its strong emphasis on speculative or metaphysical pronouncements, toward the lesser objective of more common practical educational problems and their clarification. The direction, therefore, involves a strong emphasis on analysis, both logical and linguistic, entailing considerable attention to the problems of ambiguity and vagueness, definition, claims, slogans, metaphors, and formal and informal fallacies of reasoning. In this view, the role of philosophy of education is seen as a much more modest one than examining grand aims, achieving the proper unity of theory and practice, or "making teachers good."

But what of the other side of the coin? If analysis developed as a reaction to the perceived limitations of the educationists' philosophy of education, did it tend to pursue a too arid, narrow, methodological investigation of issues? Wittingly or unwittingly, some have claimed, analysis has divorced itself from the central problems of education, including value/moral considerations, that underlie the study of education.

For example, within the decade of the 1970s, there has been a spate of scholarly criticism leveled at analysis. In 1970 Wolfe Mays wrote:

Linguistic philosophy with its emphasis on therapy, skills, language and its appeal to logic, both formal and informal, is thus as much a product of our times as earlier philosophies have been of theirs. . . . Its aim, however, has always been the negative one of showing that the philosopher can only concern himself with the form or logic of arguments, and can in no way give a direction to them. Further, by taking common sense as the criterion in terms of which our experience is to be evaluated, it ignores all the lessons we have learned as to its fallibility.[5]

In 1971 Jonas F. Soltis, generally regarded as a rigorous analytic philosopher of education, presented to the Philosophy of Education Society's membership at its annual meeting a personal, and, by his own account, "generational," critique of the recent development of analysis in philosophy of education.[6] Soltis scored analysis for employing a method inadequate for a complete theorizing in philosophy of education, insofar as analysis precludes discussion of certain kinds of philosophical questions within the realms of axiology and social philosophy.[7]

The following year Abraham Edel argued that there is a strong dissatisfaction in the philosophy of education with analysis.[8] Borrowing his title from Boyd H. Bode's "Progressive Education at the Crossroads," Edel ascribed the dissatisfaction to a weakness in analytic method itself, asserting that only a marriage among empirical and scientific studies, historical analysis, and valuation components could make such philosophy of education viable.

Subsequently, in 1975, Walter Feinberg challenged some of the claims made for "ordinary language philosophy."[9] He suggested that the major shortcomings of analysis might be found either in the methodology of ordinary language or in the result of its application. Feinberg's further criticism, perhaps more important, was that the problems of language are not coterminous with the problems of philosophy. He said:

My general inclination is to say that the method is reasonable within limits, but that it quickly degenerates when its practitioners refuse to see that the problems of language do not exhaust the problems of philosophy. For when philosophy is valued only for its prowess in clarifying linguistic muddles, then it loses its roots in the problems in men and stands to the solutions of those barriers as a barrier to be overthrown.[10]

The criticism of analysis, one must note, focuses almost entirely on the alleged inadequacy of its methodology, especially the sharp contrast drawn by analysts between empirical, analytic, preference, metaphysical, and normative statements as well as the sharp separation between doing analysis (language inquiry) and empirical inquiry. Traditionally, it is claimed by its detractors, analysis has retired from the field of philosophy of education in terms of wrestling with meaningful problems, and has left itself the perhaps necessary, but hardly consequential, tasks of clarifying meaning, noting distinctions, detecting presuppositions, and so on; in short, the attempt to achieve "clarity before commitment" by "sweeping out the stables" of philosophy of education.

In this somewhat melancholy version of analysis, it is impossible to do justice to its positive side. To counter the criticism is, I suppose, a negative approach, for a proper defense is had in showing how a position makes its distinctive contribution, not by making claims about its virtue.[11] Therefore, to get down to cases, it seems reasonable for us to address the contributions of analysis in order to see its success or failure.

ANALYSIS IN EDUCATION: THE BEGINNING

The phrase analytic philosophy of education, even within academic circles, is certainly not a commonly understood one. Neither irreverence for philosophy of education nor crude parochialism accounts for this fact. The beam of analysis has been lit in the United States for twenty years now, but how well it illuminates and what it illuminates have yet to be discussed. This effect has had an entirely unnoticed academic consequence, although some wish that, like minor earth tremors, it would be felt but pass in due time.

The first tremors to be felt in philosophy of education were largely the result of intellectual foraging expeditions on the part of academic philosophers whose analyses made landmark contributions. The efforts of philosophers such as Gilbert Ryle, R. M. Hare, and P. H. Nowell-Smith in England, and Max Black, John Hospers, and R. B. Perry in the United States are given as examples. Ryle, for instance, in *The Concept of Mind*,[12] provided educationists with scores of distinctions, detailed analyses of task verbs, and the use of sentence framing as well as a rather elegant theory of the relationship between propositional (knowing-that) and performative (knowing-how) knowledge.

The second wave of tremors was initiated by those who purposely employed analytic techniques in order to clarify educational problems. Perhaps the first effort in this respect was C. D. Hardie's book, written in 1942, *Truth and Fallacy in Educational Theory*.[13] Hardie argued:

The present state of educational theory, with its numerous conflicting doctrines, can hardly be regarded as satisfactory, and the present book is an attempt to resolve some of the disagreements. It has been customary to consider that disagreement in such a subject is quite respectable, just as it has long been considered to be respectable in philosophical theory. But recent years have seen a change in the attitude of some professional philosophers. The Cambridge analytical school, led by Moore, Broad and Wittgenstein, has attempted so to analyze propositions that it will always be apparent whether the disagreement between philosophers is one concerning matters of fact, or is one concerning the use of words, or is, as is frequently the case, a purely emotive one.

It is time, I think, that a similar attitude became common in the field of educational theory. . . .

In the succeeding pages I have attempted to do this for what are perhaps the three most typical theories of education.[14]

Hardie's book, although successful in aim, was not well accepted since it seemed to be a highly specialized and narrow analysis of educational theory (philosophy of education). Indeed, one might regard the book as falling stillborn from the press.

The effort initiated by Hardie was not taken up again until one year after the 1955 NSSE yearbook, in a landmark issue of the *Harvard Educational Review*.[15] It consisted of academic and educational philosophers' plumping for the analysis of educational problems. The trend in this direction was hastened along the following year with the publication of D. J. O'Connor's *An Introduction to the Philosophy of Education*. The author undertook to connect the analytic movement in philosophy with the philosophy of education. He contended:

Although the scope and methods of philosophy have been completely transformed in the last forty years, no attempt has been made before to relate this important intellectual revolution to the philosophy of education. In doing so, this book provides a simple explanation and illustration of what philosophy can (and cannot) do for educational thinking.[16]

O'Connor's work is a classic in the analytic approach to educational philosophy because he outlined the general features of analysis and applied the tools of analysis to such concepts as "values" and "value judgments," "educational theory," "explanations," and "morals and religion." O'Connor took a hard line with regard to the role philosophy can play in the study of education. He concluded:

. . . this means that in the present condition of human knowledge we cannot hope for more from philosophy than occasional and fragmentary glimpses of enlightenment along with a reasonable confidence that its continuous practice will keep our minds free of nonsense. But this is something very valuable that only philosophy can give us.[17]

Thus O'Connor cast grave doubt on the adequacy and validity of philosophy of education and its role in solving educational problems. He offered a limited role for philosophy of education, encouraging those so engaged to eschew philosophy of education in the "grand style."

The third wave of tremors issued from the use of analysis and its techniques by practicing philosophers of education. The trend in this direction was pushed along by a number of people, especially Israel Scheffler of Harvard, a philosopher strongly influenced by contemporary British analysis. He wrote a number of distinguished volumes and produced many outstanding students who have devoted themselves to teaching and writing about educational matters as well as producing their own doctoral students in philosophy of education.

Another influential philosopher was R. S. Peters. As in the case of Scheffler, Peters came out of academic philosophy, and, like Scheffler, Peters continues to hold a dual appointment in philosophy and education. Peters holds the chair of philosophy of education at the University of London and has devoted himself to teaching philosophy of education and producing exceptional doctoral students.

A third factor in this third wave was B. Othanel Smith of the University of Illinois. Smith was a highly competent logician and philosopher of education whose work in philosophy of education ranged quite far. In his career he emphasized that philosophy of education needed to get clearer about its aims, concerns, and manner of investigation. He opted for educational philosophy's becoming a valid and valuable study, worthy of the attention of the best minds.

There were, to be sure, other philosophers of education who saw the value of analysis and its techniques and made the great effort of getting "retooled." Some repudiated their early position while others never lost their early position entirely, but were able to appreciate the tools and encouraged their students to explore and become analytically minded.

Thus by the 1960s there was a slight but growing tendency in educational philosophy to approach educational problems within the framework of language analysis, although there was and continues to be a certain amount of controversy over the ways in which the analysis

is to be done. This controversy represents one of the methodological issues that dogs educational philosophy and comes up again and again in the literature.

This is, however, only one way to look at the methodological problem. There is also a complementary way to see things. We might note that educational philosophers other than analysts began to stress the importance of language analysis, although not accepting such basic tenets of analysis as the rejection of metaphysics and embracing the verification theory of meaning. But, informally, there was some agreement that attention had to be paid to the language of education, at least as a first step in engaging in serious work in educational philosophy.

Within the movement of analysis, however, there was further agreement that the language of education is terribly confused and misunderstood, and much of what went under the rubric of systematic and synoptic educational philosophy promoted edifices of sloganizing, leaps of blind faith, and pseudo-agreement and disagreement. Perhaps this judgment can be grasped by way of analogy. Imagine wandering into a lush natural forest filled with all kinds of colors, tangles, and shapes of things growing every conceivable way. The untrained observer sees a jungle while the naturalist sees it differently. She sees a structure to all the plants, an order to them, and can explain how each reflects dependence and independence. Analysts, like the naturalist, see the same thing about language usage, and about the possibility of making it quite understandably logical and understood. Extending the analogy a bit, without causing too great a strain, other educational philosophers have been content to observe, perhaps even enjoy, the natural forest. They have noted colors, tangles, and shapes of things without making the effort to "map the terrain." For the naturalist, the important thing about the forest is that it is highly complex but not a jungle. Analogously, for the analyst, the language of education is not a jungle; there is a lot of order. We need only to learn its structure and map it.

The use of analogy makes it possible to attempt a general account of what "counts" as mapping the terrain of the language of education. First of all, it is important to understand that analysis informs us about what *is* language use; it does not prescribe its use. Analysis thus has the function of showing that "meaning is use" or, conversely, that a belief in *real* or *true* meanings is false and misleading in the extreme. In effect, analysis divests us of misleading beliefs about language and makes us more effective in communicating clearly and truthfully.

Accordingly, a history of the contribution of analysis is necessarily rooted in how language works, what we can and cannot do with it, and what to avoid. John Wilson assigned analysis a high place in the scheme of things. He wrote:

> Within a democratic state, this duty [the ability to handle, and understand language correctly] should be even more obvious to each individual citizen. For each citizen has the power, either to add to our understanding or to add to our misunderstanding of the problems which face us; the advantages of a good system of communication, and the dangers of a bad one, are both enormously increased. We can all either contribute to our common store of acts and our logical use of them, or swell the falsehoods and the irrational appeal of propaganda, advertisement and demagogy. All the most important problems, the problems of religion, morals, politics, and sociology, can only be solved via the use of words. To understand the use of words is plainly a prior condition of solving them successfully.[18]

It may seem unnecessary to say here but it bears noting that if school personnel are to be armed with the understanding Wilson suggests, then they need to see clearly, to comprehend, what is involved in language use. In short, if teachers are to free their minds from cosmological speculations and mere verbal disputes, they need to gain a solid footing based on conceptual, language, and argument skills.

But it is also painfully obvious that many undergraduate and graduate students in education do not want the tools of clear reasoning suggested by Wilson. They want something that is emotionally gripping, with or without the corresponding thought to the analysis behind it. Rightly or wrongly, students feel they are entitled to a confrontation with broad educational issues that are in some way exciting, uplifting, and relevant.

The fact that analysis takes issue with broad issues in educational philosophy that may indeed incite in students feelings of emotion and relevance is of no mean consequence. Analysts recognize that many persons are more easily moved by sentiment than by reason, but a sentimental treatment of an educational problem or issue might also spawn vagueness, ambiguity, pseudo-explanation and agreement, vacuous principles, slogans, social engineering, and impractical prescriptions.

This last point directs attention to the next section of this article. Analysis is not a "school" of educational philosophy, at least in the traditional sense. Rather, it reflects the work of people engaged in the analysis of educational discourse in the hope that what will emerge from the effort will necessarily affect and inform educational decisions.

In a word, analysis seeks to make crystal clear those factors that are relevant to informing and enlightening a philosophy of teaching so that wise decisions in education will be made. Analysis cannot make them. Hence, in what follows are, along with skeletal arguments, three analyses that undoubtedly have had a powerful influence on contemporary educational philosophy and decision making. It is hoped that a discussion of these, however truncated by the limitation of space, will throw some light on the methods and contributions of analysis.

THREE ANALYSES

CONDITIONS OF KNOWLEDGE

The concept of knowledge has been the subject of many thorough analyses. This is because of all the concepts worthy of analysis in philosophy knowledge is certainly primary. In educational philosophy it leads directly into fundamental and far-reaching problems in curriculum as well as having a value in the formation of a coherent and useful philosophy of teaching.

Questions about the status and extent of our knowledge of the world, of ourselves, and other people—not to speak of particular branches of knowledge, like logic and mathematics—have occupied the attention of philosophers for nearly as long as philosophy itself has been in existence. The answers to such questions form part of that important branch of philosophy known as epistemology, or the theory of knowledge. Analysts, however, have been particularly interested in the conditions of knowledge, namely, what conditions anchor down knowing-that (propositional knowledge).

The traditional view of propositional knowing ("S knows that P") has been the "JTB" analysis (Justified True Belief). That is, three conditions—truth, belief, and a "rationale" or justification for the belief—anchor the conditions of propositional knowledge. However, the "JTB" formula has not escaped the ravages of counterexample or the charge of inadequacy. Hence, attempts to construct an improved analysis of propositional knowledge have usually resulted in adding a fourth condition or some sort of modification of the justification condition.

What has been important for educational philosophy is the recognition of the distinctions between "knowing that" (propositional knowledge, as in "I know that today is Tuesday"); "knowing how to" (performative knowledge, as in "I know how to swim"); and "knowing to" (dispositional knowledge, as in "I know to tell the truth").

Although the conclusion that all knowing is performative has never been completely refuted[19] it has been challenged by educational philosophers. For example, Jane Roland [Martin] argued that distinctions between types of knowing would be obscured (and pedagogically damaging) if one were to take all knowing as performative.[20] She argued that while some performances do not require practice (such as "Columbus is the capital of Ohio") other performances (e.g., swimming) do require practice. She concluded that it is legitimate to maintain the distinction between propositional and performative knowledge in terms of the "practice" criterion, even if it is not a logical distinction. Moreover, she contended that we might wish to extend the distinction to include "knowing to," since while "knowing how to" involves a performance, "knowing to" includes the performance or capacity *plus* the tendency to act. Thus, for instance, to tell the truth is not just to "know how to" tell the truth or be truth-telling, nor is it merely to "know that one should tell the truth" in response to the question: "Should one tell the truth?" Rather, it is to exhibit the "track record" of truth-telling; that is, the tendency to tell the truth in appropriate situations. In short it is to be of the disposition or proneness to tell the truth under appropriate circumstances.

What is important in the foregoing is that Roland attempted to justify a nonreductionist view of propositional knowledge based on the practice criterion and stressed the value of a pedagogical "payoff" in maintaining distinctions. In effect, she provided criteria to open up rather than close off or reduce the types of knowledge.

Now, with respect to this brief and necessarily truncated treatment of the concept of knowledge, two important points stand out. First, an understanding of the concept of knowledge is basic to any teacher, for it seems obvious that a teacher ought to know when he or she is or is not teaching knowledge. Second, although the reductionist view of knowledge is logically pure, the attempt to maintain the logical purity of knowledge seems counterproductive in a philosophy of teaching. Teachers are aware that different approaches, strategies, tactics, rewards, and the like attach themselves to teaching "know that," "know how to," and "know to." Thus analysis shows that the reduction of all knowledge to "know how to" seems unwarranted, at least for a philosophy of teaching.

CONCEPT OF TEACHING

Philosophers of education have agreed that "teaching" is a central educational concept and is badly in need of mapping. Moreover, it will be noticed that there are numerous other conceptual problems and practical issues associated with the concept of teaching, including values, learning, students' rights, and, of course, the previously discussed nature of knowledge. In the efforts to map what is commonly meant by teaching in educational discourse, it will not be necessary to examine all the issues associated with it. Suffice it to say that analysis has attempted to develop a descriptive rather than a prescriptive concept of teaching and to distinguish it from other concepts with which it is often confused.

B. Othanel Smith pointed out three ordinary uses of the word teaching.

> First, it is used to refer to that which is taught, as a doctrine or body of knowledge. . . . Second, "teaching" is used to refer to an occupation or a profession—the profession of one who instructs or educates. Finally, "teaching" is used to refer to ways of making something known to others, usually in the routine of the school.[21]

Smith's selection is instructive because it provides a start for an analysis of the verb to teach, namely, the central use of teaching: "ways of making something known to others, usually in the routine of the school."

This sense of the concept of teaching is not some easily identified process like swimming or playing tennis; one cannot easily tell from simply watching a person's behavior whether or not he or she is teaching. There is nothing, in other words, one could do that one could not do with a valid teaching intent. Whether a given act is to count as teaching depends, minimally, on a teacher, a subject matter, and a student. These three conditions "set the stage," as it were, for us to say that teaching could take place: a teacher who understands enough to lead an inquiry, a subject matter to be taught, and a potential learner of the subject matter. But is this enough? Not quite. Whether a given act is to count as teaching depends on the pattern of action and whether that pattern satisfies the intent condition. Put differently, teaching as a process involves a triadic relationship between teacher, subject matter, and student, and, in addition, whatever one is doing in teaching it seems necessary that one must reveal what it is that one intends to teach. In this fourth condition, then, not everything counts as trying to get someone (student) to learn through teaching. We can, of course, get someone to learn without teaching: by intimidation or through torture. To teach someone something depends on what one *does* in trying to teach. James B. McClellan argued:

At any given moment the intention that another learn may or may not be present to the consciousness of a person teaching; that intention may or may not be the end-in-view toward which particular acts are directed. But that intention is what gives distinctive form or character to the teaching encounter. It is strictly by reference to that intention that we can tell whether any particular action is to count as part of or a digression from the teaching itself. In short, the intention that B learn _____X is one of those intentions that figure prominently when we are deliberating about actions—deciding what to do, explaining what we've done, evaluating what happened—and that typically disappear from consciousness when we're actively engaged with the world.[22]

The last point is important. The teacher intends to bring about learning. Sometimes the teaching is successful and sometimes not. The notion of intent is critical, for if the teacher did not intend to bring about learning, what would we say? We would be confused or perplexed, because we expect teaching to have an aim or a goal. One way of making this point is to see that teaching is a *task* word. It is an activity, like searching or treating, that aims at success. Of course, learning can come about without the teacher's activity, but when the teacher teaches, she does aim at learning. However, even though the teacher intends learning, she may fail. This fact points out that the task sense of teaching does not guarantee the *achievement* sense. We all know of cases where the teacher has taught (in the *task* sense) but the student has not learned. Scheffler's analysis is helpful here:

> Clearly, if I have been teaching my nephew how to catch a baseball, he may still not have learned, and may in fact, never learn how to catch a baseball. I have of course, been trying to get him to learn how to catch a baseball, but I need not have succeeded. Generally, then, we may say that the schema "X has been teaching Y how to . . . " does not imply success. Suppose, however, that I have taught my nephew how to catch a baseball. If I have indeed taught him, then he must, in fact, have learned how. Were I to say, "Today I taught him how to catch a baseball but he hasn't learned and never will," I would normally be thought to be saying something puzzling. We may then, say that the schema "X taught Y how to . . . " does imply success. This schema represents a "success" use of "to teach" whereas the earlier schema does not, representing rather an "intentional" use of the verb.[23]

Scheffler alerts us to think of "to teach" as having the dual aspect of intent and success/failure or, as Ryle put it, task and achievement. "To teach" is thus to set about the task of producing learning, although whether one successfully achieves the intended upshot remains an open question.

The most fundamental point to be understood here is that the view that teaching *implies* learning is not necessarily true. What analysis demonstrates is that teaching does not necessarily imply learning in the task sense but does in the success sense. The clarification of the logical relationship between teaching and learning turns on the ambiguity (task/achievement sense) of the verb to teach. We should be alert to this inherent ambiguity and be on our guard to detect fallacies of equivocation that follow from it. Teaching and learning are logically independent concepts, for we can have teaching without learning and learning without teaching. Hence, any attempt to allege an implicative relationship between the two concepts is misguided. When this occurs, as is quite common, we should probably assume a prescriptive function to the dictum "No teaching without learning." However, to recognize a prescription rather than a description is perhaps necessary if we are not to be done in by the slogan.

THE CONCEPT OF EDUCATION

If any term is basic to the study of philosophy of education, it is education, since philosophy of education is the application of philosophy to education. This, then, has served as an Archimedean point for a number of analyses of the term education. We do not begin with aims of education, for what we must do, if we are to be clear, is begin at the beginning with an understanding of what the term education involves. That is, we must begin with the concept of education.

To help in this task, we will consider the work of R. S. Peters. He informed us that education picks out no particular process; rather it implies three criteria that processes must satisfy. One of these, according to Peters, is that something worthwhile should be immanent in such processes. He said that "to educate" functions logically like the expression "to reform."[24]

> Both concepts have the criterion built into them that something worthwhile should be achieved. "Education" does not imply, like "reform," that a man should be brought back from a state of turpitude into which he had lapsed; but it does have normative implications, of along a slightly different dimension. It implies that something worthwhile is being or has been intentionally transmitted in a morally acceptable manner. It would be a logical contradiction to say that a man had been educated but that he had in no way changed for the better, or that in educating his son a man was attempting nothing that was worth-while.[25]

According to Peters, then, the concept of education involves the criterion of the worthwhile. The second criterion is that of initiation of somebody into cognitive perspectives. He argued:

> We do not call a person "educated" who has simply mastered a skill, even though the skill may be very highly prized, such as pottery. For a man to be educated it is insufficient that he should possess a mere know-how or knack. He must have also some body of knowledge and some kind of a conceptual scheme to raise this above the level of a collection of disjointed facts. This implies some understanding of principles for the organization of facts. We should not call a man who was merely well informed an educated man. He must also have some understanding of the "reason why" of things.[26]

Peters's third criterion of an educational process involves that what is learned rules out indoctrination. He claimed:

> For something to count as an educational process, a minimum of comprehension must be involved. This is quite compatible with formal instruction and commands, and in this respect with indoctrination; for in methods such as these, children do understand, in an embryonic way, what is being passed on; they know what they are learning or doing and grasp the standards which they are expected to attain. Furthermore, there is a minimal sense in which they act as voluntary agents; for they can rebel and refuse to do what is required of them.[27]

Peters's analysis, then, suggests that indoctrination, really indoctrinative procedures of transmission, are ruled out of the concept of education insofar as they lack wittingness and voluntariness on the part of the learner.

In sum, for Peters there are three criteria implicit in central cases of education: its worthwhileness, its initiation into cognitive perspectives, and its ruling out of indoctrination

There are, however, a number of problems with Peters's analysis, the chief one being the claim that "to educate" functions logically like the expression "to reform," to intend something good for the student (and to achieve that intended good). There is, obviously, as Jonas F. Soltis has pointed out, one sense in which Peters's claim is true.[28] Part of the use of education is the intent to produce or achieve a good for the student. Hence, we teach subject matter and procedures because we believe such things are worthwhile or good for the student. So we do have the sense of the use of education as doing something good for somebody, at least in the judgment of the educator.

On the other hand, there are contexts in which the term education does not have the aim of the worthwhile. Soltis gives the example of studying Chinese education. The commitment to studying Chinese education does not include committing oneself to the proposition that there is something of value or worth being taught or learned in Chinese schools.[29] The mere fact that we can and do use education in a purely neutral way, as in the case of talking objectively and dispassionately about one's study of Chinese education, shows that Peters's analysis is not correct. Moreover, to make the case against the analysis even stronger, it is illustrative to note that we do talk about education in a pejorative way, totally disavowing any notion of the worthwhile, such as when we talk of "the educated fool."

The major contribution of Peters's analysis is the recognition that there sometimes is and sometimes is not a normative element attached to the term education. Moreover, it is obvious that in employing the term education it picks out no particular process. Rather, as Peters suggested, it implies criteria that processes must satisfy or conform to. This point may be appreciated by grasping the fact that when we wish to condemn teaching methods (transmission process of education) that, in our judgment, transmit material in such a way that it is objectionable, we may thunder forth, or quietly say, "This is not education, it is indoctrination (or some such thing)." In this case the choice of words proves nothing in itself other than that we are condemning something objectionable.

Hence, it is important that we remain alert to the inherent ambiguity of the term education and look askance at somebody's willingness to engage us in dispute as to whether certain teaching processes "really are" or "really are not" educative or indoctrinative. Moreover, we should look doubly askance (if that is possible) at somebody's attempt to produce a definitive definition of education because either the attempt will suffer from generality and be of little use to anybody or it will smuggle in somebody's personal judgment about what education ought to be. If one keeps these two points in mind, then one will not likely be led astray in discussions about education.

A FURTHER POINT

First the inevitable qualification. If one is of a mind to examine the contributions of analysis, then it is patently clear that the foregoing treatment of the concepts of knowledge, teaching, and education is truncated and simply will not suffice. More needs to be said. The text and periodical literature of analysis, although not immense, is sufficient to allow, with cautious confidence, the assertion that a sustained and critical examination has been initiated with regard to the employment of slogans in education;[30] the concept of equality of educational opportunity;[31] the concept of needs;[32] the concept of adjustment;[33] the concept of indoctrination;[34] the concept of definition;[35] the concept of judgment;[36] subjective conditions for an explanation;[37] metaphors in education;[38] and educational policy.[39]

The important point to be made here is that the above listing is merely a representative sampling of analyses that have been undertaken in terms of their logical consistency or inconsistency as well as their relation to educational issues.

The further point, however, that I now wish to emphasize is that analysts tend to concentrate on rather small pieces of the philosophic pie. That is, they concentrate on a continuing dialogue with regard to the above issues, believing strongly in the continuity of argument or dialogue, on the one hand, and the opening up of other lines of argument by seizing on a heretofore obscure and seemingly unimportant point that needs clarification. In either case, what is important is the additive factor; that is the contribution, no matter how small, to an educational argument. It is this element of analysis that is so appealing and intriguing.

The above point is simple, but like most simple ideas not so easily explained. The idea may be caught in the characterization of analysis suggested to me by my colleague Gerald M. Reagan. He allowed that an analyst has no good reason for not making a contribution to the literature, for analysis encourages people of even modest intelligence to select a very small or narrow problem and work toward its solution. Even a person of average intelligence, with little wit and charm, can contribute to the ongoing philosophical debate. Hence, the only possible excuse for someone's not making a contribution is fear of failure, laziness, or some such thing, but surely not a lack of intelligence.

How far have we got, then, in our presentation of the contribution of analysis? First, we looked at three concepts considered central to the study of philosophy of education and demonstrated how analysis has suggested they be considered. Second, we saw that other concepts and problems central to education have been extensively examined by analysts. Finally, we saw that the goal of analysis is the attempt to clarify a philosophic issue having to do with education, no matter how small or insignificant, in order to add to our understanding of the issue.

We can now illuminate the relationship between traditional

philosophy of education and analysis by considering that each "side," as it were, is enriched by the effort of the other. It is simply not the case that the two are incompatible and necessarily at war with one another. Common ground has been found. Recently analysts have been paying attention to the language of causality, becoming, determinism, the hidden curriculum, open classroom, and so on. Phenomenologists, for some time now, have been deeply interested in metaphorical utterances, and analysts need to pay attention to this body of literature. While it is true that the reciprocal relationship is not entirely obvious to the two sides, it is equally true that the recognition of its value will enrich both sides in the form of increased understanding and self-esteem. Only the envious scholar, if he or she cannot possess something that somebody else has, prefers that the other person not have it either.

IN CONCLUSION

Philosophy of education is, broadly speaking, a philosophical study of education. As should be abundantly clear, this enterprise depends heavily on how one views the task of philosophy. Analysis has as its *metier* the logic of whatever claims are made about the enterprise of education. What analysis does in the field of education is to examine the concepts that are central to its theory and practice. It attempts to be critical of educational concepts both singly and in relation to one another, and its goal is helping students to learn to be critical. If we think of this in terms of skills and techniques of conceptual, language, and argument analysis, then analysis does try to develop in students a critic's stance. But more than this is involved. Being clever in analysis is not equivalent to being a good critic. Being critical involves employing the tools of clear reasoning, but to learn to be critical depends as much on attitude and disposition. It is not enough to be able to detect an informal fallacy or an unwarranted assumption, and drawing attention to ambiguities and to commonplaces scarcely counts as critical thinking. What also is needed is the throwing of light on a traditional or contemporary problem of education. To show that a certain statement is on one interpretation true but trivial, on another interpretation not trivial but also not obviously true, should issue in a conclusion that might not only force but encourage the speaker to adjust her or his thinking. To *encourage* and not *force* is probably the single greatest contribution analysis might make today in educational philosophy.

Footnotes

1   *Modern Philosophies and Education*, Part I, The Fifty-fourth Yearbook of the National Society for the Study of Education, ed. Nelson B. Henry (Chicago: University of Chicago Press, 1955).

2   It is not quite clear what is meant by the term implication, especially when it is asserted that metaphysical, epistemological, or axiological beliefs contain "implications" for certain educational policies and practices. For a thorough treatment of this problem, see Hobert W. Burns, "The Logic of the Educational Implication," *Educational Theory* 14 (January 1964): 31–39. See also L. M. Brown, *General Philosophy in Education* (New York: McGraw-Hill, 1966), pp. 69–83.

3   This point was told to me in 1972 by the late Everett Kircher, a colleague at Ohio State University, who was a student of Bode and a colleague of Hullfish. Kircher suggested that Hullfish was not hostile to philosophy per se, indeed he had great respect for it, but to a type of philosophy that ignored what he considered to be the critical questions of philosophy of education.

4   The problem of implication turns up again in the "new" dress of "social/cultural philosophies." The writer most influential in declaring or staking out this position in educational philosophy is Theodore Brameld. See his *Philosophies of Education in Cultural Perspective* (New York: Dryden Press, 1955) and *Patterns of Educational Philosophy* (New York: Holt, Rinehart & Winston, 1971).

5   Wolfe Mays, "Linguistic Analysis and the Philosophy of Education," *Educational Theory* 20, no. 4 (Summer 1970), p. 283.

6   Jonas F. Soltis, "Analysis and Anomalies in Philosophy of Education," in *Proceedings of the Philosophy of Education Society*, ed. Robert D. Heslep (Edwardsville, Ill.: The Society, 1971).

7   Ibid.

8   Abraham Edel, "Analytic Philosophy of Education at the Crossroads," *Educational Theory* 22, no. 3 (Spring 1972).

9   Walter Feinberg, "The Limits of the Indoctrination Debate: Or How Ordinary Can Ordinary Language Philosophy Be and Still be Philosophy," in *Proceedings of the Philosophy of Education Society*, ed. Richard Pratte (San Jose, Calif.: The Society, 1975).

10   Ibid., pp. 21–22.

11   I am indebted to Professor J. Gordon Chamberlain for pointing this out to me in an earlier version of this paper.

12   Gilbert Ryle, *The Concept of Mind* (New York: Barnes & Noble, 1949). For the relationship between propositional and performative knowledge, see chap. 2.

13   Charles D. Hardie, *Truth and Fallacy in Educational Theory* (Cambridge, Eng.: The University Press, 1942).

14   Ibid., pp. ix–x.

15   "The Aims and Content of Philosophy of Education," *Harvard Educational Review* 26 (Spring 1956).

16   D. J. O'Connor, *An Introduction to the Philosophy of Education* (London: Routledge & Kegan Paul, 1967), book jacket.

17   Ibid., p. 45.

18   John Wilson, *Language and the Pursuit of Truth* (Cambridge: Cambridge University Press, 1967), pp. viii–ix.

19   See John Hartland-Swann, "The Logical Status of 'Knowing That,'" *Analysis*, April 1956, pp. 111–15. Hartland-Swann argued that all knowledge was essentially performative. He claimed that verbal performances were not essentially different from any other type of performance. His conclusion, although it has been challenged, has not been refuted.

20   Jane Roland [Martin], "On the Reduction of 'Knowing That' to 'Knowing How,'" in *Language and Concepts in Education*, ed. B. Othanel Smith and Robert H. Ennis (Chicago: Rand McNally, 1961).

21   B. Othanel Smith, "A Concept of Teaching" in ibid., pp. 86–87.

22   James E. McClellan, *Philosophy of Education* (Englewood Cliffs, N.J.: Prentice-Hall, 1976), pp. 36-37.

23   Israel Scheffler, *The Language of Education* (Springfield, Ill.: Charles C Thomas, 1960), pp. 42-43.

24   R. S. Peters, *Ethics and Education* (Glenview, Ill.: Scott, Foresman, 1967), p. 3.

25   Ibid.

26   Ibid., p. 8.

27   Ibid., p. 17.

28   Jonas F. Soltis, *An Introduction to the Analysis of Educational Concepts*, 2d ed. (Reading, Mass.: Addison-Wesley, 1978), pp. 12-13.

29   Ibid., p. 13.

30   For example, see B. Paul Komisar and James E. McClellan, "The Logic of Slogans," in *Language and Concepts in Education*, chap. 13; see also Scheffler, *The Language of Education*, chap. 2.

31   The concept of "equality of educational opportunity" has been quite thoroughly analyzed. Especially valuable are Myron Lieberman, "Equality of Educational Opportunity," in *Language and Concepts in Education;* Robert H. Ennis, "Equality of Educational Opportunity," *Educational Theory* 26, Winter 1976; and Brenda Cohen, "Equality, Freedom, and Independent Schools," *Journal of Philosophy of Education* 12 (1978).

32   The concepts of "needs" and the "needs curriculum" have been examined by Reginald D. Archambault, "The Concept of Need and its Relation to Certain Aspects of Educational Theory," *Harvard Educational Review* 27, Winter 1957; B. Paul Komisar, "Need and the Needs-Curriculum," in *Language and Concepts in Education;* and Alan R. White, "Needs and Wants," *Proceedings of the Philosophy of Education Society of Great Britain* 8, July 1974.

33   See, for example, C. J. B. Macmillan, "The Concept of Adjustment," in *Introduction to the Philosophy of Education*, ed. George F. Kneller (New York: John F. Wiley, 1964).

34   See Ivan Snook, *Concepts of Indoctrination: Philosophical Essays* (London: Routledge & Kegan Paul, 1972); idem, "Indoctrination and the Indoctrinated Society," *Studies in Philosophy of Education* 8 (1973); also, Robert H. Ennis, "Is It Impossible for the Schools to be Neutral?" in *Language and Concepts in Education*.

35   See Scheffler, *The Language of Education*, chap 1; also, Robert H. Ennis, *Logic in Teaching* (New York: Prentice-Hall, 1969), especially Part Two.

36   See William F. Hare, "The Teaching of Judgment," *British Journal of Education Studies* 19; and Thomas F. Green. *The Activities of Teaching* (New York: McGraw-Hill, 1971), chap. 8.

37   See Soltis, *An Introduction to the Analysis of Educational Concepts*, chap. 4.

38   Felicity Haynes, "Metaphor as Interactive," *Educational Theory* 25, no. 3 (Summer 1975); Andrew Ortony, "Why Metaphors are Necessary and Not Just Nice," *Educational Theory* 25, no. 1 (Winter 1975); Green, *The Activities of Teaching*, chap. 3; and Scheffler, *The Language of Education*; chap. 3.

39   See Thomas F. Green, "What is Educational Policy?" in *Educational Policy*, ed. Janice F. Weaver (Danville, Ill.: Interstate Printers and Publishers, 1975); also in the same volume are worthwhile articles by James E. McClellan, Mary Anne Raywid, and Myron Lieberman. See also Donna H. Kerr, *Educational Policy: Analysis, Structure, and Justification* (New York: David McKay, 1976).

Existential and Phenomenological Influences in Educational Philosophy

DONALD VANDENBERG
University of Queensland, Australia

This historical account of existentialism and phenomenology's impact on and contribution to philosophy of education in America since mid-century will begin with definitions.

The heart of existentialism is found in the 1846 motto of the first existentialist, "Subjectivity is the truth." Kierkegaard made this claim repeatedly in his *Concluding Unscientific Postscript* to emphasize inwardness, that is, that each person is inwardly aware of his own feelings, emotions, moods, desires, thoughts, volitions, projects, and goals. This inner awareness of one's own existence is the essence of the human reality. Self-conscious awareness, however, is not given but achieved. It results from reflections on the structures of what is given in existence to ascertain how they enable and limit one's project of becoming oneself. The conditions of one's own existence can be reflected on, clarified, and integrated in a gradual deepening of one's inner being. Existentialism is this reflection on the conditions of human existence in order to become an individually existing person. Its goal is to overcome alienation from oneself, or inauthentic existence, and to promote becoming oneself, or authentic existence. The connection with philosophy of education is obvious. Education is the matter of becoming who one can become.

Phenomenology also articulates the internally given structures of self-conscious awareness, but it differs from philosophy of existence in three ways: rigor, outwardness, and cognitive concern. Existentialism expresses inner awarenesses of one kind or another. Their truth remains unproven, whereas phenomenology has developed public methods to describe what is seen in the insights. Phenomenological description removes idiosyncratic elements and delineates the essential characteristics of the phenomenon that is given to consciousness, using techniques that yield intersubjectively valid results. Outwardness, a major structure of consciousness known to phenomenologists as "intentionality," is one of these central results. Paralleling Kierkegaard's "inwardness," the word "outwardness" refers to the open access to the world that haunts every waking moment and through which one knows the world. The first phenomenologist tried to establish the foundation for knowledge of the world in the laws of consciousness. Whereas existentialism emphasized the noncognitive elements of existence, Husserl tried to establish the science of universal reason. The connection with philosophy of education is obvious. Education is the matter of coming to know things and developing one's reasoning powers.

Pure phenomenology remains in the cognitive domain. The hybrid, existential phenomenology, using phenomenological method to investigate the conditions of human existence in systematic ways, includes the affective and volitional domains. Its connection with education is obvious. Education is the matter of becoming aware of one's own possibilities and of the possibilities of the world, correlatively. Education is becoming as reasonable a person as possible, given the human condition.

Existentialism strongly influenced philosophy of education for a decade after the appearance of Harper's "The Significance of Existence and Recognition for Education" in the 1955 National Society for the Study of Education (NSSE) Yearbook, *Modern Philosophies and Education*. Existential phenomenology influenced it for a decade after Vandenberg's "Existential Education and Pedagogic Authority" was read to the 1966 meeting of the Philosophy of Education Society (PES). The shift to the hybrid this paper precipitated was part of the more general reorientation of philosophy of education toward greater academic respectability.

This chronological perspective allows placing the literature that applied existentialism and phenomenology to education into seven categories.

1. Articles applying existentialism to education began to appear in 1951. They culminated in Morris's 1966 *Existentialism in Education,* one of a series that involved an already outmoded approach to philosophy of education. The nation's leading idealist in philosophy of education (Butler), its most eminent realist in education (Broudy), and most pragmatists in education no longer believed in an "ism."

2. The early sixties was a period of intense concentration on the methodology of philosophy of education. Burnett's 1961 paper in *Educational Theory* challenged the validity of drawing implications for education from a preconceived philosophical position. Among subsequent publications, a dozen exhibiting existential and phenomenological inclinations appeared from 1963 to 1967.

3. The first use of phenomenology by a philosopher in American education was Huston Smith's John Dewey Society Lecture in 1965, *Condemned to Meaning,* which was much better than a narrow-

minded review by Vandenberg in 1966 suggested. The direct use of phenomenological method in Vandenberg's 1966 paper initiated the phenomenological phase of the influence of existential thought in education, which culminated in the 1974 collaborative volume *Existentialism and Phenomenology in Education.*

4.   In his paper in that volume Vandenberg introduced hermeneutics to combine the methods of linguistic analysis and phenomenological description when doing philosophy of education, thereby fulfilling Smith's 1965 intent and the goal of Morris's 1965 PES address, and initiating the hermeneutic phase of the influence of existential thought on educational theory.

5.   Articles embodying personal scholarship in a philosopher of existence have appeared since 1962. These have elevated the general understanding of existentialism in education, but the influence is restricted to the author himself. He has merely done his homework publicly.

6.   The reviews of the literature showing the influence of existentialism in educational philosophy began in 1958.

7.   The critical literature began with Skorpen's 1964 paper on Morris in *Educational Theory.* The influence has been salutary, although restricted to the author himself. He has merely done someone else's homework publicly.

These seven categories will furnish the outline for this article, which will present fuller definitions and discuss the literature chronologically as it considers in turn the contributions to philosophy of education of existentialism, methodology, phenomenology, and hermeneutics. It will then look briefly at the scholarship, reviews, and criticism.

EXISTENTIALISM

Existentialism seems nihilistic, forever dwelling on the negative aspects of life. It is concerned with meaninglessness, homelessness, powerlessness, facelessness, normlessness, truthlessness, solitariness, and even with nothingness. It discusses contingency, accidence, purposelessness, restlessness, uneasiness, and the modern malaise of the spirit. It analyzes the moods of boredom, loneliness, nausea, anxiety, anguish, dread, and despair. It examines the phenomena of fault, guilt, sickness, suffering, tragedy, and death. In fact, Camus claimed that philosophy begins with reflections on suicide.

The gloom and doom, however, is but half the story. In Kierkegaard's words, "The genuine subjective existing thinker is always as negative as he is positive, and *vice versa.*"[1] He said the town crier of negativity falsifies existence. The negative aspects are analyzed to understand and transcend them. The experience of meaninglessness is probed to find the structure of personal significance. Conditions of homelessness are explored to prepare for homecoming. Lack of power is examined to discover the power of being. The anonymity of everyday life is described to establish the conditions for being somebody. Apartness is investigated to distinguish the incapacity to be alone from genuine solitude. The truthlessness of gossip and idle chatter is distinguished from witnessing to the truth. Normlessness is evaluated to show how it can be transcended through listening to the call to being. Nothingness is confronted to establish a project of being.

If it deals with contingency, directionlessness, and uprootedness, existentialism finds the way beyond the "absurd" world through enthusiastic engagement. The phenomena of fault, guilt, suffering, sickness, tragedy, and death are considered as limiting situations that establish the parameters of the human condition within which consummations occur. The moods of boredom, anguish, despair, nausea, and dread show the necessity for the courage to be and for the cheerfulness and serenity of authentic existence. The loss of self and the loss of community disclose the conditions for overcoming estrangement from oneself and alienation from other people. The loss of world reveals the need to regain the primordial access to the world that belongs to authentic existence. The possibility of suicide manifests the felt significance of human life.

Existentialism conquers nihilism through its elucidation of the human predicament. Being self-consciously aware of one's own existence entails awareness of both negative and positive aspects. Given situations usually have reasons for optimism and reasons for pessimism, equiprimordially. The cup is usually half full and half empty. In Kierkegaard's terms, the existing thinker is as comic as he is tragic, and as tragic as comic, or his own existence mocks him.[2]

Prior to 1966 there was no dearth of positive thinkers to praise the virtues of human progress. The impact of existentialism on philosophy of education through its negativism reoriented educational thought to greater realism. This is exemplified in the first mention in the educational literature. Although his address to PES, printed as "Education for Tragedy" in *Educational Theory* in 1951, explicitly rejected Sartre's "existentialism" in a nonbook by that name, Benne's thesis was as existentialistic as can be. Benne claimed that society was full of the stuff of tragedy, but lacked the form of tragic drama. There were moral crises galore but no tragic heroes to acquire wisdom through suffering. Willy Loman but not Oedipus. Education should abstract the dramatic form of tragedy as a model for educational endeavor. Benne's effort resembled Nietzsche's search for the Apollonian influences to calm Dionysian impulses, or Camus's claim that the more chaos threatened, the more classical one had to become. It was quite distant from the reconstructionism of the 1943 *The Improvement of Practical Intelligence* Benne coauthored and later rejected as "naive liberal-optimism." It was very close to the existential concerns of the quests for identity and community of his 1961 Bode Lectures, with which it was reprinted as *Education for Tragedy* by the University of Kentucky Press in 1967.

The second mention of existentialism, published in *Educational Theory* in 1952 by Brameld's students at New York University, was a true harbinger, for this collaborative essay was assembled by Maxine Greene. The 1954 articles by Fallico and Morris in *Educational Theory* each applied the whole ism to the whole of education, in six and twelve pages, respectively. Both were frequently quoted in Kneller's 1958 *Existentialism and Education* and in Morris's 1966 *Existentialism in Education*, the first and last books applying the ism to education. Fallico stressed the need for the creation of the self in education, and Morris applied to education the idea of freedom of choice from Sartre's popularized existentialism.

Harper's paper in the 1955 NSSE yearbook was different. He emphasized one major symptom of alienation and how education could overcome it. Showing that the aim of education is overcoming homelessness, Harper focused on the need for recognition of the pupil as an individual, as a member of society, and as a human being. Harper's emphasis on the need to develop the student's relation to the world and to truth, and on the need to know oneself and one's times to be at home in one's place on earth, showed that existentialism does not entail anti-intellectualism.

The reference to existentialism as a resource for theory building in Broudy's 1955 article in the *Journal of Philosophy*, "How Philosophical Can a Philosophy of Education Be?" may have encouraged some of the forty-odd articles on existentialism and education appearing in the next decade. Morris published another paper in 1958, Kneller's book appeared, and then one or two papers were read at PES each year. In 1974 Denton claimed that these early papers, including Vandenberg's 1962 *Harvard Educational Review* paper recommending existential education for the anesthetic society, were mostly a body of moralistic doctrine. A few titles will indicate their scope. Wirth wrote "On Existentialism, The Emperor's New Clothes, and Education" for *Educational Theory* in 1955. Morris wrote "Existentialism and the Education of Twentieth Century Man" in *Educational Theory* and Kneller had a paper on the way to appropriate knowledge in education in the *Harvard Educational Review,* both in 1961. O'Brien's "Between Two Cultures: An Existential View of Curriculum" in *School and Society* in 1961 may be the most enduring early paper.[3] Soderquist's *The Person and Education,* 1964, may be the soundest book of the first phase of the influence of existentialism in philosophy of education. Its essence as a philosophy of crisis is captured concisely in Lionel Etscovitz's paper read to PES in1969, "Martin Buber's Challenge to Educational Philosophy."

METHODOLOGY

Greene published three papers on methodology in the decade subsequent to the 1952 paper: "The Uses of Literature" in *Educational Theory* in 1957, and "Philosophy of Education and the Pseudo-Question" and "Imaginary Gardens with Real Toads in Them: The Literary Experience and Educational Philosophy," read to PES in 1960 and 1963. The first argued that imaginative literature is important to philosophy of education because it grasps the lived world. Its conclusion became the thesis of her first phenomenological paper fifteen years later: "By cultivating awareness, by keeping context and variety of perspective in mind, by consulting the widest range of experiential materials, he [the philosopher of education] may at last develop an objectivity, which is, after all, only the ability to integrate a number of points of view." The others also claim that perennial philosophical questions are genuine even if traditional answers were "pseudo." Several other papers also made recommendations pointing toward phenomenology and hermeneutics. In "Educational Theory and Inspiration" in *Educational Theory* in 1963, Phenix claimed that philosophy of education should present insightful, imaginative perspectives to generate enthusiasm and impart a sense of importance to the work of educating. The companion article by Gowin claimed that because scientific theories treated people as objects, an educational theory has to be constructed on a nonscientific model to account for the fact that educating occurs in morally guided, interpersonal action.

Butler's 1964 address to PES called for the development of a logic responsive to the flux of human existence, with features enabling it to grasp the lived world for use in educational theory. In "An Apology for Tendermindedness" at the same conference, Soderquist suggested that existential phenomena should be taken into account in education by attributing ultimate reality to the pupil as a person. The "manifesto" was Troutner's statement. Read to the same conference, "Existentialism, Phenomenology, and the Philosophy of Education" claimed (a) both existentialism and education were concerned with particular, existing individuals, and (b) phenomenology was the appropriate method for philosophy of education because the lived world was the site of education. Because phenomenological descriptions of educational phenomena would grasp education as it occurs in the lived world, it would enable educators to keep their eyes on the ball game instead of the statistics book.

In "The Role of Analysis in Educational Philosophy," appearing that same year in *Educational Theory*, Broudy claimed that important features of educational problems were disclosed by existentialists and phenomenologists, who describe phenomena as they present themselves (quoting Cairns). Similarly, Morris's 1965 address, appearing as "Detente in Educational Philosophy" in *Educational Theory*, asked for a merger between analysis and existentialism.

In *Educational Theory* in 1967 Vandenberg analyzed the problem of moral education, showing that education had to be grounded in the being of the child, and claiming that the theory of the ground ought to employ phenomenological method. Vandenberg's position paper at a conference on the role of philosophy of education in a research-oriented environment, appearing in the 1967 College of Education *Record* of the University of Idaho, was the first use of the philosophy of science of Schutz, Merleau-Ponty, Sartre, Straus, Wild, and Natanson in the consideration of the methodology of educational theory. It argued that any scientist presupposes his own wakeful access to the world, that any social or behavioral scientist also presupposes the wakeful access to the world of the subjects of his inquiry, and that teachers have to assume their students have a wakeful access to the world about which they are learning. It claimed that to grasp wide-awakeness, or consciousness, the method of educational theory should be phenomenology. These claims were documented with Schutz's "Multiple Realities" and Straus's *The Primary World of the Senses*, the former of which was to receive much emphasis in Greene's discussions of wide-awakeness in her 1973 and 1978 books. Greene's collection, *Existential Encounters for Teachers*, also appeared in 1967. It contained no selections from the phenomenologists Husserl and Schutz, and only one page from Merleau-Ponty, Greene's major resources when she entered the phenomenological phase, but it allowed teachers in training to read philosophers of existence themselves, which was very important at that time.

Questions of legitimacy were clearer after Estes specified "Concepts as Criteria Derived from an Existential Phenomenological Perspective" in *Educational Theory* in 1970. Broudy's 1970 paper, "Knowing With," brought the realm of prereflective consciousness to the attention of PES in Polanyi's "tacit knowing." This level of awareness was featured again the following year in Denton's "On the Existential Understanding of Teaching Acts." Neither Dennis's 1974 method paper in *Educational Theory* nor the papers by Carter, Troutner, and Vaughn read at the 1974 PES meeting advanced much beyond Troutner's 1964 manifesto.[4]

Near the end of his 1958 book, reprinted in 1964, Kneller said existentialism would remain relevant if it used the kind of rigor employed by Heidegger and Sartre, meaning their phenomenology.[5] Morris ended his 1958 paper in *Educational Theory* saying, "It is the grounding of pedagogy in this commitment to the transcendent possibilities of man, accessible through his freedom and choice, which characterizes the educational program of Existentialism." All possibilities are transcendent ones, gained through wakeful access to the world. The turn to phenomenology, therefore, was completely within the spirit of these two pioneers.

PHENOMENOLOGY

The early articles in existentialism and education oversimplified human reality compared with the phenomenology of the child's existence describing four stages of freedom correlative to increasing depth of consciousness presented in the 1953 translation in *Educational Theory* of Buytendijk's "Experienced Freedom and Moral Freedom in the Child's Consciousness." Using his own research and Merleau-Ponty's *Phenomenology of Perception* as resources, Buytendijk formulated pedagogic principles for educating the child up to the fourth stage of moral freedom. His theoretical complexity went unheeded until 1966, when Vandenberg's "Existential Educating and Pedagogic Authority" included a phenomenology of the child's world to establish the conditions under which the child will freely ascribe authority to the teacher. He described the pedagogic relation as it appears in the lived world, then pedagogic authority as one of its constituent elements. This manifested the phenomenon of educating within the pedagogic relation, that is, teaching as the codisclosure of possibilities of being. The phenomenological description of educating as codisclosure in Vandenberg's 1969 paper "Non-Violent Power in Education" in *Educational Theory* is the only account in the history of educational ideas of learning within the pedagogic encounter. Vandenberg's 1969 PES paper, "The Pedagogic Admonition in Existential Perspective," formulated principles of classroom management based on nonviolent power. By describing and interrelating several educational phenomena with a common language, these three papers established the pedagogic relation as the distinct form of intersubjectivity Buber claimed it to be.

Freire's description of the cointentional constitution of the pedagogic relation in the 1970 translation of *Pedagogy of the Oppressed* is independent corroboration of Vandenberg's description of genuine teaching as the codisclosure of possibilities in the world. Freire's claim that the necessary conditions of pedagogic dialogue include love, faith, hope, and humility substantiates Smith's 1965 deduction of the conditions necessary for experiencing personal significance, that is, trouble, hope, endeavor, faith, and mystery. According to Smith, a condition of the pedagogic relation was the teacher's leading a perceptibly significant life, implying that the teacher needed faith and hope. This dimension of pedagogy received elaboration in Vandenberg's paper on openness as the pedagogic atmosphere in the 1975 volume *The Philosophy of Open Education*, edited by Nyberg, which utilized Bollnow's work to describe the affective conditions necessary to constitute the pedagogic relation.

Why existentialism cannot be applied directly to education shows in what Smith said in his last chapter: "The most fundamental responsibility of education is to sustain this live invitingness the world has for children."[6] A fresh description of authentic existence in childhood and youth, focused on the quality of the world, has to be obtained to allow each phase of human existence to be lived fully. Based on Guardini's theory, this point was more fully explained in Vandenberg's "Life-Phases and Values" in *Educational Forum* in 1968.

Phenomenology cannot be applied directly to education either. Phenomenological method has to be used to describe the child's existence, the child's world, and/or something as it appears in the world of the child, that is, freedom, authority, teacher, school, and so forth. The goal is a theory of the chronological development of inwardness and outwardness, that is, of the educative evolution of conscious existence as it occurs within a person's life. The goal is a genetic phenomenology describing the educative development of a consciously existing person, a theory of ontogenesis that emphasizes the most essential characteristic of the human being, that is, the phenomenological factor.

The best American application of phenomenological method to educational theory shows how the child expands his reality through personally significant learning that promotes a fuller presence to the world. It is Philo Pritzkau's *On Education for the Authentic,* published by International Textbook Company in 1970. Pritzkau formulated an advanced dialogical pedagogy, based on Buber, that also embodies the interrelation between micro and macro meanings that he learned, like Smith, from Merleau-Ponty.

The child's world, designated as the primary world, the landscape into which one lives directly when one is in full presence to the world and wide awake, was an important focus of Vandenberg's 1971 *Being and Education.* This volume introduced the ideas of the origin of one's being, the need to return to landscape in a recovery of being, and, from Langeveld, the child's wanting to be someone. These are found in Greene's 1973 *Teacher as Stranger,* where the primary world was taken from Merleau-Ponty, as it was in her 1971 "Curriculum and Consciousness" in the *Teachers College Record.* In addition to great promise, Palermo showed how to arrange the knowledge learned in school to open up the child's world in his "Direct Experience in the Open Classroom," in his "Critical Pedagogy: The Hermeneutic Phenomenology of the Child's Lived World," and in his "Education, the Flesh, and Aesthetic Meaning," read to PES in 1974, 1976, and 1977, respectively.

Two excellent papers by Greene showed the student's consciousness had to be opened toward the world to enable academic learning to be perceptually relevant: "Towards a Reciprocity of Perspectives" read to the 1972 PES meeting, and "Countering Privatism" in *Educational Theory* in 1974. The former fully conceptualized the 1957 conclusion into an original model of learning concerned with the conscious constitution of meaning, and the latter showed how to educatively reduce alienation in the counterculture.

Greene's use of phenomenology in *Teacher as Stranger* begins with the reference to wide-awakeness and "Multiple Realities" found in Vandenberg's 1967 paper and the first chapter of *Being and Education.* It becomes more pervasive than explicit. She defined philosophy as if it were phenomenology, then began each chapter by raising prevalent definitions to explicit awareness as a prelude to examining definitions of great historical importance, which raised more sedimented meanings into explicit consciousness. This virtually puts the reader through the phenomenological reductions, prepares him for the subsequent phenomenologies of existence, knowledge, and value, and obligates him to make his own choices. The multiplicity of perspectives, however, prevented depth. The juxtaposition of passages explaining existentialism and phenomenology to the great philosophers of history made phenomenology into one ism among the others. The title shows the aim is from existentialism, that is, to encourage the teacher to be a bit of a stranger. Such a teacher would need Greene less than an understanding of homecoming as an existential possibility to assist pupils in overcoming their homelessness. Like the 1974 papers on method, the book confuses talk about phenomenology with doing phenomenology. Quoting phenomenologists is not necessarily doing phenomenology, and neither of these applies the method to a particular domain to describe the phenomena in that domain. The talk about the teacher's choices does not describe the phenomena of teaching, nor of the pedagogic relation, nor of learning. The book does not proceed from personal insight into educational phenomena to their description but goes to the literature for insights. This contrasts sharply with Husserl's motto, "To the things themselves."

In other words, the volume demonstrates that the ism had not disappeared. Morris's plea for detente was followed by greater polarization. During the fifties people assumed different philosophical beliefs and applied them to education. These were ideological standpoints, isms. During the sixties and early seventies they started out with different philosophical methods and applied them to education. These were still ideological standpoints but at the level of methodology. The polemics accordingly shifted over to methodology as a quarrel between analys*ism* and phenomenolog*ism* in a kind of reciprocating intellectual suicide.

Phenomenologism is obvious in the 1974 *Existentialism and Phenomenology in Education*, edited by Denton and published by Teachers College Press. Its very existence proves the method had become an ism in need of exorcism. The papers in it by Kaelin and Phenix were reprinted from the first phase. The paper by Collins says that the child is in the position of Schutz's stranger when he first goes to school, which is an obvious imposition on children that violates the phenomenological intent of returning to the phenomena themselves.

Troutner's paper comparing Dewey and Heidegger is still of no interest to anyone, and his paper on temporality relies on Heidegger's distinctions regarding the structure of time, which applies, if at all, only to people of Heidegger's own age when writing *Being and Time* (late thirties) because even his own thinking was time-bound. Troutner's equation of "clock time" with "objective time" errs because clock time is intersubjective time. Seconds, minutes, and hours are not objective but conventions adopted by people willing to coordinate their lives. Children have to learn the hours and to integrate personal time with intersubjective time and with the cosmic time of days, months, seasons, and years.

Denton's and Chamberlin's papers in the volume concern methodology. Denton's rejection of linguistic, substantive, and functional definitions of teaching sheds little light on what he then dared call the mystery of teaching, and the reference to hermeneutics indicated that he had already partly followed Vandenberg into the third phase of the influence of existential thought in education. Chamberlin, undecided whether phenomenology is one or many things, explained Husserl's method as if it were applicable by anyone in education. The use of Husserl's *Ideas* to explain phenomenology should be accompanied by the quest for apodictic evidence and the goal of laying the foundation for each of the special sciences distinctive of that book. In her contribution, Greene repeated the theme of her 1957 paper and justified literature in the education of everyone because of its insights into the lived world. It is worth noting that her citations continue to be negative. There are no citations of Saroyan, Wilder, *Carousel, Fiddler on the Roof, Barefoot in the Park, Prisoner of Second Avenue,* or whatever else shows life to be as comic as tragic. Broadway, Hollywood, and Shakespeare understood that comedy was as existential as tragedy. On the other hand, her mastery of phenomenological method enabled her to fully demonstrate the educative effects of literature.

Comparing the Denton volume with the writings of the fifties, or *Teacher as Stranger* with the first book in existentialism and education, shows remarkable progress. These volumes nevertheless closed the phenomenological phase of the influence of existential thought in philosophy of education as surely as Morris's volume closed the first phase. Phenomenologism had to be transcended to understand the educative development of the human being and to ground pedagogy in the conditions of human existence.[7]

HERMENEUTICS

Vandenberg did not ask about the method of philosophy, phenomenology, or philosophy of education in his paper in the 1974 volume, entitled "Phenomenology and Educational Research." To avoid the isms into which these questions lead, he asked what educational theory would be like if the theorist conceived his role like theorists in the other sciences. Each of the sciences has its own theorists who formulate the concepts and conceptual structures that outline the phenomena distinctive of the particular domain. These make it possible to conduct empirical and quantitative research into the domain's phenomena because they define them.

Applying this concept of the essence of theory to education means that the educational theorist should establish the conceptual frameworks that outline educational phenomena. After the essential characteristics of educational phenomena have been specified, empirical and quantitative research into the phenomena of education can be undertaken. The great value of the findings of research in the field of education based on the conceptual frameworks of allied social and behavioral sciences should not blur the logical distinction that these inquiries investigate the phenomena of psychology, sociology, history, anthropology, and so forth, rather than educational phenomena, and the findings are contributions to the sister disciplines, not the science of education. Educational phenomena are related to the progressive deepening, enlargement, and integration of conscious existence through learning. Learning is coming to know things, that is, becoming aware of something of which one was not previously aware. Educational phenomena are those primarily concerned with the genesis of conscious existence, that is, with increasing a person's understanding of himself and things in the world. The idea of educational theory therefore assumes there is an educative development of inwardness and outwardness at the heart of education as a process of becoming as reasonable a person as possible, given the human condition.

To maintain an I-Thou relatedness in the formulation of the theory of the pedagogic relation as a relation between two conscious beings, the theorist has to grasp the practitioner's understanding of educational phenomena and conceptualize the practical insights by using the language ordinarily used to talk about education. The theorist should use the methods of ordinary language philosophy to obtain the prephilosophical understanding of educational phenomena as they are perceived in the lived world to work out the inner sense of the language of education. To obtain the *logos* of education, that is, the logical structure of educational theory, ordinary language philosophy has to be supplemented with phenomenological method. It is not the "logic" of the word *education* but the structure of the domain of education that is needed. The logic of the concept has to be explicitly grounded in the reality of the domain comprised of educational phenomena.

For example, after Komisar's initial effort in *Educational Theory* in 1965, the analyses of the word *learning* resulted in the anomalies Soltis mentioned in his 1971 address to PES. Various analyses were indecisive about relative priorities of "learning how to" do something and "learning that" something is the case. Komisar, however, had also referred to the different modes of learning that the different senses of the word pick out. Language analysis yields clarity about the various senses in which the word *learning* is used. This uncovers the modes of learning, that is, the phenomena of learning as they manifest themselves in the lived world. Learning-how-to refers to learning by practice, and learning-that refers to learning by study, and so forth.

The theoretical gap should be filled with phenomenological descriptions to furnish statements about the essential characteristics of educational phenomena. The goal is to establish the set of "synthetic a priori" statements comprising the *logos*, or reason, of the domain of education. This would be its common sense. For example: The child needs help. The child needs education. The child needs help to become adult. Education is merely helping the child to become adult. The pedagogic relation grows out of the parental relation. Learning is becoming aware of something of which one was not previously aware. And so on. This is the use of phenomenological method necessary to make empirical inquiry into distinctly educational phenomena possible and to improve the practice of education.

If the two phases of the method of educational theory merely explicate the prephilosophical understanding of educational phenomena gained through experience, it is an interpretive process that makes the implicit understanding (or tacit knowing) as explicit as possible. The philosophical clarification of the language ordinarily used to discuss a particular phenomenon in education is an interpretive process, and so is the subsequent phenomenological description. The two methods merge as a matter of course when highest priority is given to elucidating educational phenomena themselves.

A third phase is needed to locate the well-defined phenomenon within the domain of education and evaluate its significance for the development of an integral human life. This, too, is an interpretive matter. The method of educational theory can therefore be called "hermeneutics," meaning interpretation. Previous uses of the word are not implied. The need is for a broad, indeterminate term to encompass several methods neutrally, flexibly. The need is to ascribe priority to the object of inquiry and to let the "logic" and "method" be field-dependent, as theorists in other domains do.[8] For example, the analysis of "learning" should be completed with phenomenological descriptions of the modes of learning to account for the phenomenological factor. If this requires different kinds of phenomenological methods for their proper explication as different modes of becoming aware of something new, it should be determined within the explication itself, guided by the phenomena themselves as they manifest themselves in the course of inquiry. Anything less prescribes a priori validity to a method and involves it in an ideological ism. This then prescribes to the phenomenon, telling it what it ought to be. Nothing is less scientific. For example, theorists have often decided to call "learning" only that which their preconceived method allowed them to investigate, which prohibited the phenomena of learning from manifesting themselves. Giving priority to educational phenomena themselves may be the most important contribution that phenomenology can make to philosophy of education.

The idea of the hermeneutic of education expressed in the paper in the Denton volume partly described Vandenberg's earlier efforts to come to grips with real educational problems, using whatever theoretical tools were available. The several modes of interpretation were combined in the logical, phenomenological, and ideological analysis of homogeneous grouping in education in his 1967 "Educational Policy and Ideology" in the first issue of the *Journal of Educational Thought*. In "School Rules and Their Enforcement in Analytic/Existential Perspective" in *Educational Theory* in 1972, Vandenberg supplemented Peters's justification of punishment with phenomenological aspects of moral experience to establish the conditions under which punishment, if justified on other grounds, could also be educative. Similarly, Scudder supplemented Scheffler's rule model of teaching with Buber's existentialism in his 1971 PES paper "Initiation through Dialogue, a Model for Education."

Linguistic and phenomenological methods were combined in three of Vandenberg's papers since the Denton volume. In the previously cited paper on the pedagogic atmosphere, the usages "learning climate," "educational atmosphere," "open," and so forth, were analyzed, and the phenomena of the emotional tone of the classroom necessary to establish the pedagogic relation were then described. In an address to PES in 1975 entitled "Education and the American Dream," Vandenberg made an ordinary language distinction between "believing" and "believing in" to analyze talk about Dr. Martin Luther King's dream to obtain the conditions for ascribing believing in a "dream." Then he adapted Freire's phenomenology of the oppressed consciousness to recommend a form of political education to restore believing in the American Dream. In the bicentennial issue of the *UCLA Educator* devoted to minority group education, Vandenberg coauthored "Educational Justice" with Richard Gordon. They criticized standard interpretations of equal opportunity in education to justify a human rights view of distributive justice in education based on the individual's claim to be able to use his developmental time for his maximal humanization to fulfill his right to be. Each of these used ordinary language philosophy to grasp relevant aspects of the problem in the lived world and then phenomenological method to deal with the educational phenomena and to explicate a solution that would promote human existence. The solutions did not come from preconceived isms but from the description of the educational phenomena involved and from the goal of educational practice, that is, promoting educational value. In the paradigmatic paper on openness, for example, the search for the pedagogic atmosphere was primarily concerned with affectivity, but only for the sake of promoting cognitive learning, that is, greater educative value in classroom instruction.

The use of both existentialism and analysis in her early papers showed Greene's larger interpretive intent, which was also manifested in the use of literature in most of her writings, especially in *Teacher as Stranger*. Her shift to hermeneutics in her 1978 volume, *Landscapes of Learning*, published by Teachers College Press, is shown in her interpretation of Wordsworth's return to nature as a return to original landscape and to himself in explicating *The Prelude* in her opening essays. The application of this return to landscape and to oneself to education is reminiscent of Stenzel's interpretation of the German youth movement as recounted in Vandenberg's *Being and Education* to indicate the importance of continuous contact with landscape in education to prevent alienation from the world. This mutual use of the idea of landscape as the origin of one's being shows how intersubjectively valid results can be obtained in the hermeneutic phenomenology of education. Greene's innovative idea is that encounters with works of art enable a student to return to his original landscape and recover his presence to himself. She also extended the use of hermeneutics to a general method of learning, distinguished by a return to landscape and to oneself in a process of consciousness raising. This was recommended in women's education to overcome the alienation of childhood sexist education. Finally, she used hermeneutics to "demystify" the language regarding equal opportunity as school policy (again), showing how teachers, too, could use it to disencumber themselves of untenable beliefs about schooling. Because of the constant reference to the role of landscape in restoring one's presence to oneself but not to the presence to the world, the use of the word *landscape* is a bit of mystification for the idea of perceptual reality. Similarly, the idea of wide-awakeness permeating some chapters needs more original explication because Schutz did not use it in an educational context or it is a mystifying barrier to transparency regarding presence. The correlative presence to oneself and to the world of the child's present moment of wide-awakeness might require the greater emphasis on the presence to the world found in the last chapter of Pritzkau's *On Education for the Authentic*. Alienation from the world as well as from oneself can be overcome through placing as much importance on the educative development of outwardness as on inwardness, on consciousness as on self-consciousness.

SCHOLARSHIP

The earliest paper about a philosopher of existence by a philosopher of education was "Kierkegaard's Levels of Existence" in the first volume of *Philosophy and Phenomenological Research* in 1941 by Harry Broudy. Broudy also reviewed the translations of Kierkegaard for that journal in 1945, 1948, and 1956. In the second review he said, "Existentialism is at its best at diagnosis. Cure is another matter." This is implied in his 1961 paper in the *Journal of Philosophy* refuting "Kierkegaard on Indirect Communication."

It can be claimed that the most thorough embodiment of existentialism in educational philosophy occurred in Broudy's 1961 *Building a Philosophy of Education*. His education for self-determination, self-realization, and self-integration was strongly influenced by Kierkegaard's levels of existence and his claim that one had to remain in dialectical relation with the universal to develop inwardness and to become an individual person. Broudy's "homework," done with John

Wild in the thirties, strongly influenced who he became, and this unique person wrote the philosophy of education distinguished by his name. His subsequent abandonment of its neo-Aristotelian framework suggests that the metaphysics was not an essential characteristic of the educational theory. Deciding whether the structure of knowledge in the school curriculum represents the structure of reality before or after investigation was not as important to education as the claim that the self should be filtered through knowledge in its educative development. This is much closer to Kierkegaard than is the pseudo-existentialism that would filter the knowledge acquired in school through the self. The latter would not promote the self-transcendence that is an essential characteristic of authentic existence, but Broudy's view would.

Broudy is a paragon of how existential philosophy can affect educational philosophy: through the education of the philosopher himself. Another valuable example in which the ideas of Kierkegaard were cited in the context of an educational problem, not because the author favored him but because they were both relevant and true, is Pai's "The Free Will Problem and Moral Education" in *Educational Theory* in 1966.[9]

REVIEWS OF THE LITERATURE

Neither Smith and Stanley's "The Historical, Philosophical, and Social Framework of Education" in the 1956 *Review of Educational Research* nor McCaul's 1958 review in that same journal mentions Benne's 1951 address or the report of Brameld's seminar. McCaul mentioned the 1954 and 1955 articles and Harper's paper. In the 1961 review in that journal, Clayton said the influence of existential thought on philosophy of education was largely indirect. He cited Broudy's criticism of Dewey's problem solving in the 1960 *Bulletin* of the School of Education at Indiana University as an example of the indirect influence and questioned the scholarly status of direct approaches. In the 1964 article in the same journal Kneller explained how two of his articles focused on existential rather than educational categories. In the 1967 review in that journal, Wheeler said, "There is in much of the literature a certain failure of sustained grasp of existentialism in its many manifestations that must be regarded as a defect." In a review of the literature read to PES in 1967, Morris mentioned the impact of existentialism on school counseling and teaching theory, then cited some papers on method to reiterate his desire for a merger of language analysis and existentialism.

CRITICISM

Constructive criticism occurred when someone seriously studied an existential philosopher, then eruditely showed how someone else did not. One example will show the futility of the *genre*. In a 1972 *Educational Theory* article, Kestenbaum corrected Troutner's misunderstanding of Heidegger, this century's most profound philosopher of existence. The journal's readers who had read Heidegger already knew the point and others were unable to ascertain the truth. It is more productive to write a relevant exposition, for example, Khoobyar's excellent paper on the "Educational Import of Heidegger's Notion of Truth as Letting Be" read at the 1974 PES meeting.

One adversary criticism deserves consideration. A 1977 PES paper entitled "The Poverty of a Phenomenology of Education" referred to Tesconi's *Schooling in America*, Troutner's 1974 method paper, Chamberlin's 1969 *Toward a Phenomenology of Education*, and Greene's *Teacher as Stranger*, none of which pretended to contribute to a phenomenology of education, but it neglected the riches of Pritzkau, Freire, and Vandenberg, all of whom did contribute to a phenomenology of education. It also neglected to mention Chamberlin's 1971 and 1972 PES papers, "An Educational Occasion" and "Expectation in Education," and Greene's 1972 and 1974 papers, "Towards a Reciprocity of Perspectives" and "Countering Privatism," and chapter seven of her book. Each of these riches contributed to a phenomenology of education and refutes the critic. He also cited Palermo's 1974 PES paper but neglected to mention six other papers heavily indebted to phenomenology, read at the same conference, and published in the same proceedings he consulted for Palermo's paper, namely, the Khoobyar paper; Carter, "Philosophical and Psychological Theories of Phenomenology"; Scott and Collins, "Two Types of Educational Dialogue"; Stott, "The Myth of the Born Teacher"; Vandenberg, "The Pedagogic Atmosphere"; and Vaughn, "Fundamental Value Conflicts in Education: Toward Reconciliation."

In other words, the critic cited virtually none of the vast body of relevant literature, not even when it was very close at hand, and he cited Tesconi, Troutner, Chamberlin, and Greene once each. In truth he criticized but one paper and surrounded it with misquotations that failed to justify the broadside condemnation of the approach. Had his paper been entitled "The Poverty of Palermo's Phenomenology of Education" to reflect its true scope (he wanted to refute a particular phenomenology of education, i.e., Palermo's), its own poverty would have been obvious. The reasons for its egregious card stacking appears in its penultimate sentence: "As a devout philosophical realist I must confess that I have never had either the patience, the interest, or the stamina to plod through the abstruse metaphysics of Husserl." He did not read Husserl because he was a "devout philosophical realist," which is not explained.

The critic's refutation of the "straw man" revived the worst of the old ism approach, the poverty of which was recognized throughout the field in the early sixties. Since then there have been no confessing realists in philosophy of education, devout or otherwise.

On the other hand, the two realists who wrote in the 1955 NSSE yearbook had extremely favorable attitudes toward phenomenology. John Wild, who wrote the main article on realism in the yearbook, also published an article in the first issue of *Philosophy and Phenomenological Research* in 1940, "The Concept of *the Given* in Contemporary Philosophy." It concluded, "Employing the method of phenomenological description, he [the true empiricist] dwells on each appearance, whatever it may be, trying to lay bare its structure or *logos*."[10] Wild expanded this statement in a 1943 article in that journal, "On the Nature and Aims of Phenomenology." There he said, "This twofold purpose, to describe *the actual structure* of *what actually appears* is clearly indicated in the word phenomenology itself, the *logos* or structure of the concrete or material phenomena."[11] It set this definition into context when he added, "Philosophy must be phenomenological in this sense, for it must be both true to the given data, and structurally articulated. . . . Philosophy is neither appearance alone, nor logos alone, but phenomenology, the logos of the phenomena."[12]

The favorable attitude toward phenomenology of the other person writing as a realist in the NSSE yearbook, Broudy, was already discussed.

The phenomenological description of the essential characteristics of educational phenomena discloses phenomena out there in the world, not "in" consciousness. This is as realistic as one can get, philosophically speaking. The critic's main point was fear that cognitive learning processes in school would be individualized away. When the same point was made of the early existentialists, Vandenberg introduced phenomenological method to overcome the solipsism of the pseudo-existentialists. Then when it became a relevant point of criticism of phenomenological psychology in education, Vandenberg introduced the hermeneutic method to circumvent the solipsism of the pseudophenomenology of humanistic psychology in education. His shorter version of the 1974 hermeneutics paper, read to PES in 1973 and accessible to the critic, anticipated his point when recommending the use of ordinary language philosophy to insure that the phenomenology of education described educational phenomena as they appear in the lived world, that is, in the real world prior to its reconstruction by the imaginative, explanatory theories of the human sciences. The compatibility with Husserl's plan is evidenced in the following passage from his "last great work," *The Crisis of European Sciences and Transcendental Phenomenology:* "For the life-world— the 'world for us all'—is identical with the world that can be commonly talked about. . . . Thus the world is always such that it can be empirically, generally (intersubjectively) explicated and, at the same time, linguistically explicated."[13] This is not "abstruse" or "metaphysical."

The viability of a phenomenology of education is not at question. It would be a mistake to fall into phenomenologism to respond to criticism from an ideological standpoint. The task is to come to grips theoretically with three things. First, the kind of learning at the heart of educating—becoming aware of something new. Second, the kind of person at the heart of education—a conscious being concerned with his own educative becoming. Third, the pedagogic relation as the distinct form of interhuman relation that is deliberately established to enable human beings to come into being through disclosure of their possibilities of being. The task is to understand how to promote the humanization of the young, to learn how to educate them to become as reasonable as possible, given the human condition, and to formulate a theory that does not explain away the joys and struggles that adult human beings have when raising their young to enter into the responsible existence appropriate to the mature members of the species. One has to claim theoretical autonomy from all other disciplines, and from pseudophilosophical prejudices, to formulate the theory of education that delineates the phenomena of education. The literature that has made progress toward achieving recognition of this goal is not without its proper value.

Footnotes

1 Sören Kierkegaard, *Concluding Unscientific Postscript*, trans. D. F. Swenson and W. Lowrie (Princeton, N.J.: Princeton University Press, 1968), p. 78.

2 Ibid., p. 81.

3 Others include J. Killinger, "Existentialism and Human Freedom," *English Journal* 50 (May 1961): 303-12; N. Gayer, "Will Existentialism Triumph over Pragmatism?" *Phi Delta Kappan* 43 (October 1961): 20-24; N. Gayer, "Existentialism and History," *Social Education* 25 (December 1961): 398-400; W. O'Neill, "Existentialism and Education for Moral Choice," *Phi Delta Kappan* 46 (October 1964): 48-53; R. D. Mosier, "From Doing to Being," *Educational Theory* 15 (January 1965): 35-38; J. Scudder, "Kierkegaard and the Responsible Enjoyment of Children," *Educational Forum* 30 (May 1966): 497-503; M. Greene, "Art and the Existential Moment," *Teachers College Record* 67 (April 1966): 503-07; M. Greene, "Technology and the Human Person," *Teachers College Record* 69 (January 1968): 385-93; C. H. William, "Toward a More Existential Methodology in American Education," *Catholic School Journal* 68 (September 1968): 38-40; W. J. Stein, "Exploiting Existential Tension in the Classroom," *Teachers College Record* 70 (May 1969): 747-53; R. C. Emery, "Existentialism in the Classroom," *Journal of Teacher Education* 22 (Spring 1971): 5-9; H. S. Rosenblatt, "Martin Buber's Concepts Applied to Education," *Educational Forum* 35 (January 1971): 215-18; H. Gordon, "Existential Education as Expressed in the Hasidic Stories of Martin Buber," *Religious Education* 29 (September 1974): 579-92; and G. Matoot, "In Search of a Philosophical Context for Teaching Composition," *College Composition and Communication* 27 (February 1976): 25-31.

4 Other papers include H. Winthrop, "Methodological and Hermeneutical Functions in Interdisciplinary Education," *Educational Theory* 14 (April 1964): 118-27; G. H. Bantock, "Educational Research: A Criticism," in his *Educational Values* (London: Faber & Faber, 1965), pp. 153-74; M. Langeveld, "Some Recent Developments in Philosophy of Education in Europe," in *Philosophy and Education, Proceedings of the International Seminar* (Toronto: Ontario Institute for Studies in Education, 1966), pp. 81-101; R. Dale, "Phenomenological Perspectives and the Sociology of Education," *Educational Review* 25 (June 1973): 175-84; and D. E. Griffiths, "Individual and Organization: A Theoretical Perspective," *Educational Administration Quarterly* 13 (Spring 1977): 1-18.

5 George F. Kneller, *Existentialism and Education* (New York: Philosophical Library, 1958), pp. 143-44.

6 Huston Smith, *Condemned to Meaning* (New York: Harper & Row, 1965), p. 86.

7 Other materials of the second phase include R. Snyder, "Toward Foundations of a Discipline of Religious Education," *Religious Education* 62 (September 1967): 394-404; E. Schaffer, "Alienation and the Sociology of Education," *Educational Theory* 20 (Spring 1970): 121-28; P. Phenix, "Transcendence and the Curriculum," *Teachers College Record* 73 (December 1971): 271-83; G. Lesnoff-Caravaglia, *Education as Existential Possibility* (New York: Philosophical Library, 1972); O. F. Bollnow, "Encounter and Education," *Educational Forum* 36 (March 1972): 303-12, and 36 (May 1972): 465-72; P. Freire, *Education for Critical Consciousness* (London: Sheed and Ward, 1974); H. G. Ruthrof, "Reading Works of Literary Art," *Journal of Aesthetic Education* 8 (October 1974): 74-90; and L. Jacobs, "Existential Phenomenology and Personal Writing," *College Composition and Communication* 26 (October 1975): 293-97.

8 S. E. Toulmin, *The Uses of Argument* (Cambridge: Cambridge University Press, 1958), pp. 234, 250, 255.

9 The range of scholarship shows in a listing of the articles published in *Educational Theory*: M. Friedman, "Martin Buber's Philosophy of Education," *Educational Theory* 6 (April 1956): 95-104; A. Wirth, "Viktor Frankl and the 'Responsible Self'," *Educational Theory* 12 (October 1962): 241-46; K. Winetrout, "Buber: Philosopher of the I-Thou Dialogue," *Educational Theory* 13 (January 1963): 53-57; D. E. Denton, "Albert Camus: Philosopher of Moral Concern," *Educational Theory* 14 (April 1964): 99-102; G. Y. Koos, "The Structure and Process of Self," *Educational Theory* 14 (April 1964): 111-14; J. C. Willers, "Unamuno Centennial," *Educational Theory* 15 (October 1965): 312-20; B. F. Baker, "Existential Philosophers on Education," *Educational Theory* 16 (July 1966): 216-24; B. V. Hill, "Sören Kierkegaard and Educational Theory," *Educational Theory* 16 (October 1966): 344-53; J. Mullins, "The Problem of the Individual in the Philosophies of Dewey and Buber," *Educational*

Theory 17 (January 1967): 76–82; J. W. Hillesheim, "Action and Solitude: A Nietzschean View," *Educational Theory* 19 (Fall 1969): 357–62; H. S. Broudy, "Sartre's Existentialism and Education," *Educational Theory* 21 (Spring 1961): 155–77; G. H. Douglas, "Heidegger on the Education of Poets and Philosophers," *Educational Theory* 22 (Fall 1972): 443–49; T. Oliver, "Camus, Man and Education," *Educational Theory* 23 (Summer 1973): 224–29; K. Benhamida, "Sartre's Existentialism and Education: The Missing Foundations of Human Relations," *Educational Theory* 23 (Summer 1973): 230–39; J. Hillesheim, "Nietzsche Agonistes," *Educational Theory* 23 (Fall 1973): 343–53; E. Rosenow, "What is Free Education? The Educational Significance of Nietzsche's Thought," *Educational Theory* 23 (Fall 1973): 354–70; D. C. Williams, "Ressentiment and Schooling," *Educational Theory* 26 (Winter 1976): 72–80; T. M. Riordan, "Karl Jaspers: An Existentialist Looks at University Education," *Educational Theory* 26 (Winter 1976): 53–71; and R. Hughes, "Education and the Tragic Sense of Life: The Thought of Miguel de Unamuno," *Educational Theory* 28 (Spring 1978): 131–38.

10 J. Wild, "The Concept of *the Given* in Contemporary Philosophy," *Philosophy and Phenomenological Research* 1 (September 1940): 82. Emphasis his.

11 J. Wild, "On the Nature and Aims of Phenomenology," *Philosophy and Phenomenological Research* 3 (September 1943): 85. Emphasis his.

12 Ibid., p. 86.

13 E. Husserl, *The Crisis of European Sciences and Transcendental Phenomenology*, trans. D. Carr (Evanston, Ill.: Northwestern University Press, 1970), pp. 209–10.

References

Existentialism

Benne, K., "Education for Tragedy," *Educational Theory* 1 (November 1951): 199–210 and 1 (December 1951): 274–83.

Brameld, T., ed. "Existentialism and Education, A Collaborative Essay," *Educational Theory* 2 (April 1952): 80–91.

Fallico, A., "Existentialism and Education," *Educational Theory* 4 (April 1954): 166–72.

Morris, V. C., "Existentialism and Education," *Educational Theory* 4 (October 1954): 247–58.

Harper, R., "The Significance of Existence and Recognition for Education," in *Modern Philosophies and Education*, ed. J. Brubacher (Chicago: University of Chicago Press, 1955), pp. 215–53.

Wirth, A. G., "On Existentialism: The Emperor's New Clothes, and Education," *Educational Theory* 5 (July 1955): 152–57.

Kneller, G. F., *Existentialism and Education* (New York: Philosophical Library, 1958; reprinted. New York: John Wiley, 1964).

Morris, V. C., "Freedom and Choice in the Educative Process," *Educational Theory* 8 (October 1958): 231–38.

Kneller, G. K., "Education, Knowledge, and the Problem of Existence," *Harvard Educational Review* 31 (Fall 1961): 427–36.

Morris, V. C., "Existentialism and the Education of Twentieth Century Man," *Educational Theory* 11 (January 1961): 52–60.

O'Brien, D. W., "Between the Two Cultures: An Existential View of Curriculum," *School and Society* 59 (November 1961): 402–05.

Vandenberg, D., "Experimentalism in the Anesthetic Society: Existential Education," *Harvard Educational Review* 32 (Spring 1962): 155–87.

Soderquist, H. O., *The Person and Education* (Columbus, Ohio: Merrill, 1964).

Morris, V. C., *Existentialism in Education* (New York: Harper & Row, 1966).

Benne, K. D., *Education for Tragedy* (Lexington: University of Kentucky Press, 1967).

Etscovitz, L., "Martin Buber's Challenge to Educational Philosophy," *Philosophy of Education 1969* (Edwardsville, Ill.: Philosophy of Education Society, 1969), pp. 113–19.

Methodology

Broudy, H. S., "How Philosophical can Philosophy of Education Be?" *Journal of Philosophy* 52 (October 27, 1955): 612-22.

Greene, M., "The Uses of Literature," *Educational Theory* 7 (April 1957): 143-49.

——, "Philosophy of Education and the 'Pseudo-Question'," *Proceedings* of the 16th Annual Meeting of the Philosophy of Education Society (Lawrence: University of Kansas, 1960).

Burnett, J. R., "Observations on the Logical Implications of Philosophical Theory for Educational Theory and Practice," *Educational Theory* 11 (April 1961): 65-70.

Gowin, D. B., "Can Educational Theory Guide Practice?" *Educational Theory* 13 (January 1963): 6-12

Greene, M., "Imaginary Gardens with Real Toads in Them: The Literary Experience and Educational Philosophy," *Proceedings* of the 19th Annual Meeting of the Philosophy of Education Society (Lawrence: University of Kansas, 1963), pp. 170-84.

Phenix, P. H., "Educational Theory and Inspiration," *Educational Theory* 13 (January 1963): 1-5.

Broudy, H. S., "The Role of Analysis in Educational Philosophy," *Educational Theory* 14 (October 1964): 261-69.

Butler, J. D., "Preface to a Logic," *Educational Theory* 14 (October 1964): 229-54.

Soderquist, H. O., "An Apology for Tendermindedness," *Proceedings* of the 20th Annual Meeting of the Philosophy of Education Society (Lawrence: University of Kansas, 1964), pp. 67-71.

Troutner, L., "Existentialism, Phenomenology, and the Philosophy of Education," *Proceedings* of the 20th Annual Meeting of the Philosophy of Education Society (Lawrence: University of Kansas, 1964), pp. 118-24.

Morris, V. C., "Detente in Educational Philosophy," *Educational Theory* 15 (October 1965): 265-72.

Greene, M., *Existential Encounters for Teachers* (New York: Random House, 1967).

Vandenberg, D., "The Role of Philosophy of Education in a Research-Oriented Environment," *College of Education Record* (University of Idaho, 1967-68), pp. 22-30.

Broudy, H. S., "On 'Knowing With'," *Philosophy of Education 1970* (Edwardsville, Ill.: Philosophy of Education Society, 1970), pp. 89-103.

Estes, C. R., "Concepts as Criteria Derived from an Existential-Phenomenological Perspective," *Educational Theory* 20 (Spring 1970): 150-56.

Denton, D. E., "On the Existential Understanding of Teaching Acts," *Philosophy of Education 1971* (Edwardsville, Ill.: Philosophy of Education Society, 1971), pp. 162-71.

Carter, J. E., "Philosophical and Psychological Theories of Phenomenology," *Philosophy of Education 1974* (Edwardsville, Ill. Philosophy of Education Society, 1974), pp. 137-47.

Dennis, R., "Phenomenology: Philosophy, Psychology, and Education," *Educational Theory* 24 (Spring 1974): 142-54.

Troutner, L., "Toward a Phenomenology of Education: An Exercise in the Foundations," *Philosophy of Education 1974* (Edwardsville, Ill.: Philosophy of Education Society, 1974), pp. 148-64.

Vaughn, W., "Fundamental Value Conflicts in Education: Toward Reconciliation," *Philosophy of Education 1974* (Edwardsville, Ill.: Philosophy of Education Society, 1974), pp. 127-35.

Vandenberg, D. "Making Sense out of Existential Thought and Education," *Philosophy of Education 1974-1975* (Tempe: Arizona State University Press, 1975) pp. 23-36.

Phenomenology

Buytendijk, F. J. J., "Experienced Freedom and Moral Freedom in the Child's Consciousness," *Educational Theory* 3 (January 1953): 1-13.

Smith, H., *Condemned to Meaning* (New York: Harper & Row, 1965).

Vandenberg, D., "Existential Educating and Pedagogic Authority," *Philosophy of Education 1966* (Edwardsville, Ill.: Philosophy of Education Society, 1966), pp. 106-11.

———, "Life-Phases and Values," *Educational Forum* 31 (March 1968): 293-302.

———, "Non-Violent Power in Education," *Educational Theory* 19 (Winter 1969): 49-57.

———, "The Pedagogical Admonition in Existential Perspective," *Philosophy of Education 1969* (Edwardsville, Ill.: Philosophy of Education Society, 1969), pp. 81-87.

Freire, P., *Pedagogy of the Oppressed,* trans. M. B. Ramos (New York: Herder and Herder, 1970).

Pritzkau, P., *On Education for the Authentic* (Scranton, Pa.: International Textbook, 1970).

Chamberlin, J. G., "An Educational Occasion: A Preliminary Phenomenological Analysis," *Philosophy of Education 1971* (Edwardsville, Ill.: Philosophy of Education Society, 1971), pp 225-33.

Greene, M., "Curriculum and Consciousness," *Teachers College Record* 73 (December 1971): 253-69.

Vandenberg, D., *Being and Education* (Englewood Cliffs, N.J.: Prentice-Hall, 1971).

Chamberlin, J. G., "Expectation in Education," *Philosophy of Education 1972* (Edwardsville, Ill.: Philosophy of Education Society 1972), pp. 307-16.

Greene, M., "Towards A Reciprocity of Perspectives," *Philosophy of Education 1972* (Edwardsville, Ill.: Philosophy of Education Society, 1972), pp. 275-84.

———, *Teacher as Stranger* (Belmont, Calif.: Wadsworth, 1973).

Denton, D. E., ed., *Existentialism and Phenomenology in Education* (New York: Teachers College Press, 1974).

Greene, M., "Countering Privatism," *Educational Theory* 24 (Summer 1974): 209-18.

Palermo, J., "Direct Experience in the Open Classroom: A Phenomenological Description," *Philosophy of Education 1974* (Edwardsville, Ill.: Philosophy of Education Society, 1974), pp. 241-54.

Vandenberg, D., "The Pedagogic Atmosphere," *Philosophy of Education 1974* (Edwardsville, Ill.: Philosophy of Education Society, 1974), pp. 101-14.

Palermo, J., "Critical Pedagogy: The Hermeneutical Phenomenology of the Child's Lived-World," *Philosophy of Education 1976* (Edwardsville, Ill.: Philosophy of Education Society, 1976), pp. 92-103.

———, "Education, The Flesh, and Aesthetic Meaning," *Philosophy of Education 1977* (Urbana, Ill.: Educational Theory, 1977), pp. 315-23.

Curtis, B., and W. Mays, *Phenomenology and Education: Self-Consciousness and Its Development* (London: Methuen, 1978).

Hermeneutics

Komisar, B. P., "More on the Concept of Learning," *Educational Theory* 15 (July 1965): 230-39.

Vandenberg, D., "Ideology and Educational Policy," *Journal of Educational Thought* 1 (April 1967): 38-50.

Scudder, J., "Initiation through Dialogue, A Model for Education," *Philosophy of Education 1971* (Edwardsville, Ill.: Philosophy of Education Society, 1971), pp. 72-80.

Soltis, J. F., "Analysis and Anomalies in Philosophy of Education," *Philosophy of Education 1971* (Edwardsville, Ill.: Philosophy of Education Society, 1971), pp. 28-46.

Vandenberg, D., "Schools Rules and Their Enforcement in Analytic/Existential Perspective," *Educational Theory* 22 (Spring 1972): 192-207.

———, "Hirst, Hermeneutics, and Fundamental Educational Theory," *Philosophy of Education 1973* (Edwardsville, Ill.: Philosophy of Education Society, 1973): 302-16.

———, "Phenomenology and Educational Research," in *Existentialism and Phenomenology in Education,* ed. D. E. Denton (New York: Teachers College Press, 1974), pp. 183-220.

———, "Education and the American Dream," *Philosophy of Education 1975* (Edwardsville, Ill.: Philosophy of Education Society, 1975), pp. 298-312.

———, "Openness: The Pedagogic Atmosphere," in *The Philosophy of Open Education*, ed. D. Nyberg, (London: Routledge & Kegan Paul, 1975), pp. 35–57.

———, and R. Gordon, "Educational Justice," *UCLA Educator* 19 (December 1976): 51–57.

Greene, M., *Landscapes of Learning* (New York: Teachers College Press, 1978).

Scholarship

Broudy, H. S., "Kierkegaard's Levels of Existence," *Philosophy and Phenomenological Research* 1 (March 1941): 294–312

———, "Kierkegaard on Indirect Communication," *Journal of Philosophy* 58 (April 27, 1961): 225–33.

———, *Building a Philosophy of Education* (Englewood Cliffs, N.J.: Prentice-Hall, 1961).

Pai, Y., "The Free Will Problem and Moral Education," *Educational Theory* 16 (April 1966): 135–50.

Scudder, J., "Freedom With Authority: A Buber Model for Teaching," *Educational Theory* 18 (Spring 1968): 133–42.

Khoobyar, H., "Educational Import of Heidegger's Notion of Truth as 'Letting Be'," *Philosophy of Education 1974* (Edwardsville, Ill.: Philosophy of Education Society, 1974), pp. 47–58.

Martin, F. D., "Heidegger's Being of Things and Aesthetic Education," *Journal of Aesthetic Education* 8 (July 1974): 87–105.

Reviews of the Literature

Stanley, W. O., and B. O. Smith, "The Historical, Philosophical and Social Framework of Education," *Review of Educational Research* 36 (June 1956): 308–22.

McCaul, R. L., "Historical and Philosophical Foundations of Education," *Review of Educational Research* 23 (February 1958): 5–15.

Clayton, A. S., "Philosophy of Education," *Review of Educational Research* 31 (February 1961): 20–37.

MacMillan, C. J. B., and G. F. Kneller, "Philosophy of Education," *Review of Educational Research* 34 (February 1964): 22–61.

Morris, V. C., "Recent Literature on Existentialism and Education—A Review," *Philosophy of Education 1967* (Edwardsville, Ill.: Philosophy of Education Society, 1967), pp. 274–80.

Wheeler, J. E., "Philosophy of Education," *Review of Educational Research* 37 (February 1967): 2–20.

Criticism

Kestenbaum, V., "Phenomenology and Dewey's Empiricism; A Response to Leroy Troutner," *Educational Theory* 22 (Winter 1972): 99–108.

Scudder, J., "Why Buber Would Not Endorse a Pseudo-Existentialist," *Educational Theory* 25 (Spring 1975): 197–201.

Silk, D. N., "The Poverty of a Phenomenology of Education," *Philosophy of Education 1977* (Urbana, Ill.: Educational Theory, 1977), pp. 222–30.

Whatever Happened to John Dewey?

JOE R. BURNETT

University of Illinois, Urbana-Champaign

John Dewey's hardly is the classroom name it was for almost the first half of this century in America; and, certainly, it is not the almost household name it was during the two turbulent decades after World War II when Dewey and his purported followers were featured in the mass media as being to American education almost what the communist menace was to American culture—an association that today sounds weird unless one remembers that both phenomena stemmed from a massive conservative-reactionary tide during the period.

That tide has abated somewhat, and the educational reforms and innovations it spurred have in the last two or three decades had their day in court. And, since they were in some cases specifically predicated on being antithetical to Deweyan themes, it is interesting to see that what is happening adversely in American educational practice today cannot be charged to John Dewey and his purported followers.

This essay ranges rather far and wide in discussing "whatever happened to John Dewey." I intend the use of the term *essay* in its etymological sense, a personal summing up of a state of affairs in a manner to be accepted only as exploratory and provisional, because I am convinced that most perspectives on the role of John Dewey in American education are very partial and/or very distorted.

DEWEY, PRAGMATIC PROGRESSIVISM, AND ROMANTIC PROGRESSIVISM

The most common answer to the title question of the essay is, John Dewey was never well or widely understood. Why this was so generally elicits one or both of two further answers: His followers distorted his thought and/or he expressed himself unintelligibly.

About Dewey's unintelligibility, I have no comment beyond the fact that a substantial number of people do seem to find him very intelligible, even quite clearly profound, and they carry on intelligible

Appreciation is expressed to Patricia Amburgy, Geoffrey Lasky, Ralph Page, Jonas Soltis, and Paul Violas for helpful comments on an early draft of this essay. Appreciation is also expressed to The Center for Dewey Studies, Southern Illinois University, for permission to quote from the works of John Dewey.

discussions about Dewey among themselves. There *are* many others, however.

As for Dewey's thought having been distorted by his followers: The worth of this contention rests, I think, on what one would have expected the proper receipt of Dewey's thought to have been.

If one accepts John Dewey as the "father," "grandfather," or "elder statesman" of progressive education, and the progressive educators as the interpreters and appliers of his theory, then his thought was grossly distorted.

This is a well "received" doctrine, I think; and, since progressive education has in recent decades come to be associated with the period from the end of World War I to the end of World War II, and specifically with the Progressive Education Association (PEA), 1919–1955, then it does make a certain *sort* of sense to connect the towering figure of Dewey during that period with progressive education.[1]

But I believe this historical view is an aberration in the history of ideas, and tracing out why it is an aberration can possibly suggest a very dangerous thing about a certain strand of American educational thought.

I suggest another point of view, one that was in fact well known several decades ago when some of the people who wrote on the history of education were better trained philosophically. It is that John Dewey's contributions to educational thought were not made until the cluster of ideas forming progressive education was already well grounded intellectually and widely in circulation. Some argue that Dewey's impact was not massively felt until after 1919, as a result of the 1916 publication of *Democracy and Education* and the 1919 formation of the PEA,[2] but consider the following accounts of progressivism in education:

> The term Progressive Education took on its present defined status with the organization of the Progressive Education Association. . . . The movement itself is, however, much older, as well as much broader and deeper.

> It seems historically justifiable to say that this movement began with Rousseau (1712–1778) and the *Emile* (1762). But it was Pestalozzi (1745–1827), much influenced by Rousseau and the general humanitarian stirring of his day, who began the significant remaking of the school along the lines here under study. His influence was world-wide and reached America through many channels in the remaking of arithmetic and geography, in the making of our graded schools (coming by way of Prussia especially through the work of Horace Mann), in Sheldon's "object

lessons," and in the later influence of Herbart (1776–1842) and Froebel (1782–1852), both of whom studied with Pestalozzi.[3]

Not a few progressives find philosophical support for their educational convictions, not so much in pragmatism as in romantic naturalism. For them the main tenets of progressive education take root, not in Dewey and his followers, but in Rousseau and his adherents. Pragmatists like Dewey ground the main progressive tenets of interest and freedom in the theory of knowledge. The activity program which embodies these tenets is basically a method of testing the truth. The romantic followers of Rousseau, on the other hand, ground the tenets of progressive education principally in a theory of human nature. Since the child is spontaneously self-active, interest and freedom follow as the chief vehicle of self-expression.

The romantic naturalist has a profound reverence for nature as witness the famous assumption of Rousseau's that child nature is good, rather than fallen, as was the habit with his contemporaries. The implication here is that human nature develops according to laws as inexorable as those which heavenly bodies obey in their orbits. The duty of educators is to learn what these laws are. Once found out, it is their further duty to invoke, rather than interfere with, their operation. From this origin, then, stems the whole child-study movement. Child nature becomes the norm.[4]

What seems to be the case, then, is that progressive education early was two distinctive *philosophic* trees, not one tree with two roots—as it was *politically*. Brubacher calls these the pragmatic and the romantic naturalistic.[5] The latter, by most accounts, began to "phase into" American education as early as Horace Mann's and Henry Barnard's work around the 1840s and was dominant certainly by the time of Dewey's first well-known excursions into pedagogical theory—just prior to his Chicago years (1894–1904).

On this basis, Dewey can be seen as "throwing in" with the romantics for politico-educational purposes (e.g., overthrowing bad features of "traditional" education); and, if this is correct, then we would expect to find his criticism of his allies more muted than that of the common enemy (traditional education). The latter is in fact what we do find: He criticizes the romantic aspect of the "new" education early, and "progressive" education (which is what the new education came later to be named) late. Both early and late, traditional education was seen as the greater enemy than romanticism.

The point, however, is that Dewey entered a well-defined stream of educational thought rather than initiating it. He was accepted by the romantics, who picked and chose willy-nilly from his thought to justify their theories and practices, but it would be a mistake to think that they ever were Dewey's *followers* philosophically. And, as indicated, Dewey seemed to tolerate this.

The pragmatic and *genuine* followers of Dewey's thought are capable of explanation only on an individual basis. There is not one bit of doubt (in my mind, at least) that William Heard Kilpatrick, John L. Childs, R. Bruce Raup, George S. Counts, Harold Rugg, Theodore Brameld, Kenneth Benne, B. Othanel Smith, William O. Stanley, and Ernest Bayles (to mention widely read followers) all laid down or presupposed the pragmatic criterion as basic to their philosophizing. Each did it in an original way, and some of them perhaps did distort it on occasion—but not fully in the direction of romanticism.[6]

Dewey and the above-mentioned followers in pragmatic progressivism might appear to constitute a large and formidable group, but some of the followers were not to find a large measure of recognition until the late 1920s and the 1930s, some not until later still. Of the alternatives to traditional education, romantic progressivism was entrenched in the hearts and minds of many elementary school people well before the turn of the century, and it was to flourish among many of those same school people who were called on to provide the public school personnel and ideologies for the massive development of secondary education in America between 1880 and 1915.[7]

I think that this view of progressive education—as having two strands philosophically, but usually working as one politically against traditional education—can have certain salutary effects. Certainly, to me, it suggests how some writers perhaps get things turned around. When, for instance, Patricia Graham writes that progressive educators "conceived themselves to be acting according to the dictates of Dewey, but they applied Dewey's eclectic, imprecise, and multiple dicta to problems in which they were most interested,"[8] we can suspect that the problem is not so much with Dewey after 1900—whose pragmatic followers, above, did not find him significantly imprecise or eclectic, *or* his multiple dicta unsystematic—as it is with romantic progressives who found congenial aspects of his thought other than the basic, philosophic ones.

Not the least of the salutary things the view can provide is an ability to detect what I earlier alluded to as "a very dangerous thing about a certain strand of American educational thought." Now, initially, romantic progressivism had fairly well-developed philosophies behind it, but (1) they were not consistent with each other, and (2) even the inconsistent philosophies largely dropped out during the 1940s and 1950s as being irrelevant to American industrial and secular society. Apparently what has remained, for the most part, are lay addicts to romanticism, people who will seize almost any notion that can be used to exalt the nativistic, emotive character of the child's nature—and even if this requires ignoring other notions that might be systematically related to them but that seriously qualify them. Thus, over the years, one can find these progressives using without qualms tenets drawn from such varied intellectual resources as certain psychoanalytic thinkers, certain cognitive psychologists, certain humanistic psychologists, and even certain existentialists.

The fact that Dewey's thought (*or* the thought of other systematic thinkers) gets indiscriminately jumbled into congeries is insignificant by comparison with the dangers of the resulting view's being deficient to suggest or guide consistent research, conducive to faddism and intellectual disrespect, and perhaps, one of these days, susceptible to accepting new ideas via its romanticism, which will color it authoritarian.[9]

DEWEY AND AMERICAN EDUCATIONAL PRACTICE

How widely did Dewey's philosophy directly and consistently influence American educational practice?[10] There really is no way of knowing with exactitude; but, one suspects, very little, due to the fact that romantic progressivism seems to have been (and be) the variety of progressivism that has imbued almost all but technically trained, philosophic progressives. When, to quote Graham again, it is claimed that "Progressive educators were mainly responsible for the tremendous changes that took place in American schools between 1920 and 1950,"[11] we can have reason to doubt that Dewey's direct influence was heavily felt in a manner consistent or consonant with his philosophy.

But there is another reason for being skeptical; and that is simply the fact that Dewey's particular brand of pedagogy probably could not have been widely applied in the schools of the period—or now, for that matter. Teachers were not trained for it, schools did not have the resources for it, parents and politicians would not have stood for it. Dewey expects of teachers, for example, that they know their subject matters almost as experts know them, although teachers do not need to be researchers generating expert knowledge.[12] Teachers must also know the individual children in the classroom, and in terms of their backgrounds in the community occupations and life. Only when these things are well known can the teacher take on his or her distinctive function, that of psychologizing the subject matter so that it is warmly or enthusiastically seized by the student as relevant to his or her own level and type of problem solving.[13] This hardly was the sort of thing teachers were taught to do in the normal schools of the early 1900s; it also was hardly the sort of thing that could occur in the jam-packed classrooms and schools at that time.

What, then, the reader is likely to ask, about Dewey's Laboratory School at the University of Chicago and its supposedly wide emulation? What about the schools Dewey lauds in his and Evelyn Dewey's *Schools of Tomorrow?*[14]

About the first of these: Dewey argued against generalizing the work of the Laboratory School simply because it *was* a laboratory school and an experiment.[15] Moreover, there probably were few places that had the resources to emulate it effectively.

Now the schools of *Schools of Tomorrow* are, in various senses and degrees, "experimental" in Dewey's use of the term. But not one of them is thoroughgoing in that meaning of experimentalism. Some of them, indeed, are only marginal in preparing their students for full participation in community and occupations. Each is an example of experimentalism in some way: None is fully or predominatly experimental—certainly not in both class activities and community involvement.

What I am saying goes beyond this, however. I am saying that no matter how desirable Dewey's pedagogy might have been adjudged, it simply was not widely feasible, save that educators had secured immensely greater resources of talent, training, and hardware. That Dewey knew this is indicated, for instance, when he wrote as late as 1938 (at age seventy-nine) that

> the general principles of the new education do not of themselves solve any of the problems of the actual or practical conduct and management of progressive schools. Rather they set new problems which have to be worked out on the basis of a new philosophy of experience. The problems are not even recognized, to say nothing of being solved.[16]

Thus, even Dewey himself did not argue that his desired impact had been made, or that it would be made easily.

DEWEY ON SCHOOLING, POST-WORLD WAR I

Something else was happening to John Dewey after 1919 that bears very special comment, and that ties in with some of the above views.

Dewey made a lot of, and commentators about him make a lot of, his almost boundless faith in education as the sine qua non of democracy in an age of science, technology, and industrialization. This faith must be looked upon very closely after World War I, for it has almost disappeared with respect to education in America and particularly in the American school; whereas, up until that time, the promise of American education and schooling seemed to be one of the best reasons for his faith in education in general.

Here again, most educators lost sight—if they ever caught sight fully—of what was happening to Dewey; and, even today, some of them seize on Dewey's optimistic remarks in such a way as to mask the fact that he was on occasion very pessimistic and critical indeed. Some of his remarks are worth quoting at length in order to firmly establish this claim. Note that all except the first of the quotations are from the period of the 1930s, when progressive education supposedly was having great influence in the schools; that is, his criticism hardly is *merely* of traditional education.

> Our schools send out men meeting the exigencies of contemporary life clothed in the chain-armor of antiquity, and priding themselves on the awkwardness of their movements as evidence of deep-wrought, time-tested conviction.

> The other way in which schooling fosters an undiscriminating gulping mental habit, eager to be duped, is positive. It consists in a systematic, almost deliberate, avoidance of the spirit of criticism in dealing with history, politics and economics. . . . The school is even more indurated from a frank acknowledgement of social ills than the pulpit—which is saying a good deal. And like the pulpit it compensates for its avoidance of discussion of social difficulties by sentimental dwelling upon personal vices.[17]

Or,

> In the degree in which mere force is restored to, actual consequences are themselves so compromised that the ends originally in view have in fact to be worked out afterwards by the method of experimental intelligence.

> In saying this, I do not wish to be understood as meaning that radicals . . . have any monopoly of the use of force. The contrary is the case. The reactionaries are in possession of force, in not only the army and police, but in the press and the schools. The only reason they do not advocate the use of force is the fact that they are already in possession of it, so their policy is to cover up its existence with idealistic phrases—of which their present use of individual initiative and liberty is a striking example.[18]

Or,

> There [once] was a modicum of knowledge or information acquired in the school, but it wasn't connected; and I fear isn't much connected with how government is actually run, with how parties are formed and managed, what machines are, what gives machines and political bosses their power. In fact, it might be dangerous in some cities if pupils in the schools were given not merely a formal and anatomical knowledge about the structure of the government but also acquired an understanding of how the government of their own community is run through giving special favors and through dealings with industrial powers.[19]

Or, again,

> The number in high schools and colleges has increased sixfold and more in a generation. This irruption is something unprecedented in the history of any nation. It members proceed from those who do not have the background, tradition, or needs of the class to which the old system catered. New studies and courses are brought in as a response to their needs. But they are brought in piecemeal, without a unified aim. And the old studies persist, with little modification, side by side with the new ones. Only those pupils who have a strong natural bent come out with any clear idea either of their own capacities or of the world in which they are to live. The schools are a drift rather than a system.[20]

And, again,

> We are unfortunately familiar with the recent racial intolerance of Germany and Italy. Are we entirely free from that racial intolerance, so that we can pride ourselves upon having achieved a complete democracy? Our treatment of the Negroes, anti-Semitism, the growing (at least I fear it is growing) serious opposition to the alien immigrant within our gates, is, I think, a sufficient answer to that question. Here, in relation to education, we have a problem. What are our schools doing to cultivate not merely passive toleration that will put up with people of different racial birth or different colored skin, but what are our schools doing positively and aggressively and constructively to cultivate understanding and good will which are essential to democratic society? . . . I know that in many respects our public schools have and deserve a good reputation for what they have done in breaking down class division, creating a feeling of greater humanity and of membership in a single family, but I do not believe that we have as yet done what can be done and what needs to be done in breaking down even the ordinary snobbishness and prejudices that divide people from each other, and that our schools have done what they can and should do in this respect.[21]

And, finally,

> That the schools have mostly been given to imparting information ready-
> made, along with teaching the tools of literacy, cannot be denied. The
> methods used in acquiring such information are not those which develop
> skill in inquiry and in test of opinions. On the contrary, they are positively
> hostile to it. They tend to dull native curiosity, and to load powers of
> observation and experimentation with such a mass of unrelated material
> that they do not operate effectively as they do in many an illiterate person.
> The problem of the common schools in a democracy has reached only its
> first stage when they are provided for everybody. Until what shall be taught
> and how it is taught is settled upon the basis of formation of the scientific
> attitude, the so-called educational work of schools is a dangerously hit-or-
> miss affair as far as democracy is concerned.[22]

Generally overlooked also is the fact that Dewey gradually lost faith
in both the motivation and the ability of teachers to change the
character of American schooling. He was not highly critical of them;
but, still, one should compare his later statements with his optimistic
ones about teachers as movingly expressed in *My Pedagogic Creed,* and
in the stirring "call to arms," "Why I Am a Member of the Teachers
Union."[23]

Dewey's dour comments about education in post–World War I
America were a part of his increasingly bitter attacks on American class
society and sociopolitical rule by selfish, vested-interest groups in
politics, business, and industry. One suspects that most educators
were too tame to follow him in this direction, for all of the tempest that
George S. Counts stirred up with his *Dare the Schools Build a New
Social Order.*[24] The teachers were pretty firmly under the control of
school boards and business-type administrators, and there is little
obvious political zest evidenced by educational leaders at any time—
much less the times of the periodic Red scares, between 1920 and, well,
today.

Dewey's whole social philosophy had changed significantly, and it
could not countenance the type of corporate society into which most
educators rather blithely continued to inculcate children. The Dewey
of early Hegelian affinity seems clearly a "statist," but not so the Dewey
of the post-1900s.[25] The statement about the schools' being a "tool of
the state," above, almost sounds Marxist. Indeed, socioeconomic class
analysis was one of Dewey's common techniques, although he
supplemented it with other techniques—and roundly condemned
Marxism for its failure to see other social variables than that of class.[26]

Few followers of Dewey probably recognized how greatly he had changed, and probably few would have followed him had they. Many continued to think of him as supporting the school as an embryonic community within the late nineteenth-century communal neighborhood and extended family. But Dewey had early seen that community's limitations. He had noted the positive virtues of science, technology, and industrialization in actually breaking down these limitations, and by 1916 could remark:

> Persons do not become a society by living in physical proximity, any more than a man ceases to be socially influenced by being so many feet or miles removed from others. A book or a letter may institute a more intimate association between human beings separated thousands of miles from each other than exists between dwellers under the same roof.[27]

There is a recent view that Dewey overtly or covertly fostered corporateness in American society. This argument hinges on an equivocation: Dewey favored more centralized mechanisms for representing the social welfare interests of publics as a means of checking and cutting back centralized selfish, vested-interest controls identified with the business-industrial corporate state. *This* type of positive, publicly responsible corporateness he sees as releasing people from bureaucracy, not enslaving them to it: "A measure of the goodness of a state is the degree in which it relieves [the individual] from the waste of negative struggle and needless conflict and confers upon him positive assurance and reinforcement in what he undertakes."[28] The state, then, is to be a political provision for opportunity, one that in no wise is to interfere with the bonds of intimacy that are the basis of *social* groupings. "Thus it happens that the state, instead of being all absorbing and inclusive, is under some circumstances the most idle and empty of social arrangements."[29] Even Dewey's ideal of "The Great Community" cannot legitimately impinge on the generic bonds of social intimacy:

> The Great Community, in the sense of free and full intercommunication, is conceivable. But it can never possess all the qualities which mark a local community. It will do its final work in ordering the relations and enriching the experience of local associations. The invasion and partial destruction of the life of the latter by outside uncontrolled agencies is the immediate source of the instability, disintegration and restlessness which characterize the present epoch.[30]

Earlier it was commented that parents and politicians would have not countenanced Dewey's theory applied to pedagogical practice. This is one reason why: It directly challenges the sovereignty of the state, and it did that during times when nationalistic jingoism was rampant.

DEWEY AND EDUCATION TODAY

The general conclusions I draw are that Dewey's educational philosophy seldom was applied, seldom was understood. Its confusion with romantic progressivism still abounds, and that intellectually inchoate congeries of ideas is both significant cause and effect of educational drift.

Fred M. Hechinger recently called for political unity in defense of public education in America.[31] Lawrence Cremin raised the perspective that educational progressivism might be resurgent if another reform era emerged in America.[32] It just might be that Dewey's philosophy and philosophy of education could be offered as candidates at such a time. But, to be effective, that would mean that romantic progressivism would have to be kept intellectually and practically distinct, and Dewey's own theory would have to be far more systematically understood and better interpreted than it is today.

While there are no significant signs that the former is happening, there are some signs that the latter is. Jo Ann Boydston and Kathleen Poulos, writing in *Checklist of Writings about John Dewey*, remark that

> in the eighty-six year period covered by the first edition, more than 2,200 studies were written about Dewey and his work, an average of some 25 a year. But in the four years from January 1973 to January 1977, well over 300 items appeared, an average of more than 60 a year. However, numbers alone do not tell the whole story of the increasing attention paid to Dewey; the quality and extensiveness of the research and writing also continue to grow.[33]

Another interesting phenomenon is the extensiveness of translations of Dewey's work into a host of foreign languages. Several decades ago the translations were largely of his educational writings—themselves mainly pre-1920 publications; more recently they extended to the mature publications in formal philosophy and sociopolitical philosophy.[34]

If I am not mistaken, and picking up on Boydston and Poulos's remark, the most significant thing happening in recent Dewey scholarship is its growth in quality while it also advances in quantity. It probably is correct that researchers have had to be more highly motivated in scholarship to pursue Dewey studies during a period when his work has been relatively unpopular; but certainly it also is true that the possibility of dealing with the immense corpus of his work has for the first time been rendered less than Herculean. The credit for this goes largely to Southern Illinois University at Carbondale, whose Center for Dewey Studies dates back to 1960 as a resource and coordinating center for Dewey students and scholars internationally. The accomplishments and activities of the center would require an article to describe;[35] suffice it to say that it houses virtually all of Dewey's published writings, houses the largest collection of his correspondence and memorabilia, has now published eleven volumes of Dewey's early publications in a definitive edition approved by the Modern Language Association (the only edition of an American philosopher's works to receive such august approval), has in production several additional volumes in the envisioned series of roughly forty chronologically arranged volumes of Dewey's works, has published the *Guide* featuring articles and bibliographies by significant topic areas of Dewey's interests,[36] has published a volume with the most complete listing anywhere of both published and unpublished articles about Dewey,[37] makes small but significant grants and awards for Dewey research, and carries on a vast correspondence to aid scholars' research worldwide.

Also aiding research and indicating the interest in Dewey is the apparent fact that commercial publishers today are keeping many more volumes of Dewey's various writings in print than two or three decades ago. Several anthologies of Dewey's works have appeared in recent years, as have several analyses of Dewey's philosophy by highly recognized American philosophers.[38] George Dykhuizen's acclaimed biography of Dewey, *The Life and Mind of John Dewey* (which now has gone into a widely distributed paperback edition), is especially noteworthy.[39]

Still the corpus of Dewey writings is vast. In academic philosophy, which has moved heavily into analytic philosophy, continental philosophy, and philosophy of science since World War II, there is some renewed interest in American philosophy, and particularly pragmatism. Too often, however, academic philosophers tend to view the pragmatists—mainly Peirce, James, Mead, Dewey—rather as a firm of tailors, each responsible for one part of a jacket.[40] Needless to say, one can no more get a seamless coat of philosophic learning from Dewey in this manner than he or she can get a seamless coat of his educational philosophy from him by confusing him with romantic progressives—or other pragmatic progressives, for that matter. (And, of academic philosophers and Dewey, Garry Brodsky recently wrote an article that will interest readers of this one, addressing himself in part to the question of why ". . . if Dewey was, as Scheffler claims, 'the giant of the pragmatists,'. . . hasn't more attention been given to him and why hasn't he made more of an influence in American philosophy?"[41])

One particularly noteworthy trend in Dewey studies has been that associated with "revisionism" in the history of education. Insofar as Dewey is concerned, the debate has centered on whether or not Dewey's concepts and actions did (as the revisionists argue) or did not (as an assorted group of others argue) either covertly or overtly support conservative or illiberal sociopolitical policies in the post-1916 decades.[42] I think it too early to say what the shape of this debate will take—or, indeed, if it will be sustained. Certainly, however, it has had the salutory effect of making educational philosophers and others pay closer attention than ever before to Dewey's sociopolitical writings and activities.

CONCLUSION

I conclude with a brief statement of my own perspective on what is both wrong and needed in scholarship on Dewey's educational writings.

It seems to me that almost every account of Dewey's educational philosophy suffers from what, for a philosopher, can be called the layman's historical fallacy. By this I mean that the concepts dealt with are those that emerged, *as* they emerged, in Dewey's major *volumes* primarily on education. And when the educational volumes diminish—after *Democracy in Education* (1916), with the exception of the rather technical, specialized *Toward a Science of Education* (1929)[43] and the largely redundant *Experience and Education* (1938)— it is as though Dewey had nothing further to say.

But it seems to me that the more correct way to proceed, philosophically or conceptually, is by systematically organizing Dewey's mature philosophy and then adding and organizing all prior to that which fits consistently and consonantly.

There is more to it than this, of course, but let me indicate at least three significant things that probably would happen.

First, the lay historical method of starting with Dewey as a Hegelian organicist almost invariably begs the question about his later position. Those who start with it will trace it all the way through, becoming insensitive to where and how it drops out philosophically.[44] If one begins with the mature philosophy, the question is not begged, because there is no significant Hegelian organicism in the mature works: What is found is where it dropped out and where it early was full blown.

Second, the poverty of experimentalism as an educational philosophy is announced by its very label: It is in the early Dewey, and (I would say) in his pragmatic followers, too narrowly or exclusively a scientific emphasis. It is not until the late 1920s or early 1930s that Dewey is to emphasize that aesthetic experience is fundamental in scientific inquiry itself. The mature Dewey had an aesthetic theory and a comprehensive "naturalistic humanism" (as he styled his philosophy then, as opposed to the narrower "pragmatism" or "instrumentalism," one observes) to which the theory of scientific inquiry is conceptually adjudicated.[45] So likewise should the pedagogical "complete act of thought" or "problem solving method" be adjudicated in the way in which educators utilize Dewey's notion of inquiry.

Third, Dewey's theory of religious experience largely remains to inform his conception of education. Indeed, because his major work on religious experience, *A Common Faith*,[46] is so brief—and so acerbic on the subject of religions (in sharp contrast to the relig*ious*)—it can be the case that the work has caused us to fail to recognize how importantly religious experience figures for Dewey in other of his mature philosophical writings.[47] In any event, this aspect of Dewey's thought could be most suggestive to us today, when religious education is swelling to vast proportions as an alternative to public education—no doubt for antidemocratic reasons, in part, but perhaps in part simply because public education never has found a way to legitimately and adequately deal with religious experience as a phenomenon of ordinary experience. This emphasis on religious experience, like the one on aesthetic experience, must be "read back into" the concepts of the earlier-formulated educational philosophy if the latter is to be as comprehensive and vital as Dewey would intend—and implicitly intended—it to be.

Footnotes

1   Lawrence A. Cremin's widely acclaimed *The Transformation of the School* (New York: Alfred A. Knopf, 1961) perhaps has fostered more of an identification between the PEA and progressivism in education than its author intended. Cremin enters qualifications that do *not* allow the identification; still, the work does seem to err in emphasis. Paul Nash alone, of the reviewers of Cremin's work, seems to note this overemphasis of the PEA. See his "The Strange Death of Progressive Education," *Educational Theory* 14, no. 2 (April 1964): 65–75, 82.

Patricia A. Graham, in *From Arcady to Academe: A History of the Progressive Education Association, 1919–1955* (New York: Teachers College Press, 1967), at one point goes so far as to say that "the widespread assumption that during its lifetime the PEA represented the progressive movement is a valid one" (p. 145). This seems a gross oversimplification or reductionism in an otherwise excellent volume: Progressive education was part of a wide stream of reform progressivism that emerged in the post-Civil War period and continues (much diminished) to this day. Educational progressivism had, especially between 1919 and 1955, multifarious connections outwards with law, politics, government, and social work that were not embodied by the PEA. The progressive movement was (and is) a vastly complex phenomenon. See, for example, Frederick R. Lynch's "Social Theory and the Progressive Era," *Theory and Society* 4, no. 2 (Summer 1977): 159–210.

2   See, for instance, Maxine Greene's summary account, "Dewey and American Education," in *John Dewey: Master Educator*, ed. William W. Brickman and Stanley Lehrer, 2nd ed. (New York: Society for the Advancement of Education, 1961), pp. 86 ff.

3   William Heard Kilpatrick, "Progressive Education," *Encyclopedia of Modern Education* (New York: Philosophical Library, 1943), p. 612.

4   John Brubacher, *Modern Philosophies of Education* (New York: McGraw-Hill, 1950), pp. 305–06. Brubacher cites Rousseau's *Emile* and Froebel's *Menschenerzieung* as the classic statements of the romantic position. My colleague Harry S. Broudy notes that he well could have added Pestalozzi's *How Gertrude Teaches Her Children*.

5   In what follows, I use the expressions "pragmatic progressivism" and "romantic progressivism." Brubacher's expression "romantic naturalism" is adequate at best to label Rousseau's thought: Pestalozzi, Froebel, and almost all of the other early romanticists had undergirding theological or metaphysical support in theistic or deistic idealism.

For the purpose of this article, "romantic" and its variants will refer to a position that stresses as basic the volitional aspect of the child—through will, feeling, and imagination—as natively generative of the good person and citizen independently of any pronounced formal or academic training. To a large extent, many recent "deschoolers" fit into this position. See Sidney Hook's discussion of some modern writers (Paul Goodman, Ivan Illich, John Holt, Jonathon Kozol, and others) "who either profess themselves inspired to some degree by the thought of John Dewey or are commonly regarded by the educational public as continuing his influence" (p. 89) ("John Dewey and His Betrayers," in *Education and the Taming of Power* [LaSalle, Ill.: Open Court, 1973], pp. 89–107). Several other chapters in the volume also have excellent accounts of Dewey and his thought.

"Pragmatic progressivism," by contrast, will be taken to refer to the position that literal meaningfulness is one of the major goals for the good person or citizen; and, consequently, native tendencies should be encouraged to develop toward disciplined and precise marshaling of data for formation and testing of hypotheses. In the arts, encouragement is toward the skilled or disciplined control of qualities directly, as opposed to indirect symbolic control in science and science-like endeavors. See, for instance, Dewey on "doing, data, and science" in *Democracy and Education* (New York: Macmillan, 1916), chaps. 14 and 17, for the simplest exposition regarding science; and chap. 4 ("The Act of Expression") of *Art as Experience* (New York: Minton, Balch, 1934), regarding artistic endeavors.

6   Of the people mentioned, Kilpatrick is the one that I have most often heard depicted as being fundamentally romantic rather than pragmatic, and responsible for thus distorting Dewey's teachings to thousands of students and readers. I do not find this depiction of Kilpatrick very surprising when considering some of his discussions of "the whole child," "child centeredness," and the "project method." However, Dewey was to remark (perhaps because he had heard such characterizations) that Kilpatrick had "never fallen victim to the one-sidedness of identifying progressive education with child-centered education" (John Dewey, "Introduction," in Samuel Tenenbaum, *William Heard Kilpatrick: Trail Blazer in Education* [New York: Harper, 1951], p. viii). Certainly the characterization cannot hold one of Kilpatrick's best-known statements of his position, "Philosophy of Education from the Experimentalist Outlook," in

Philosophies of Education, Part I, The Forty-first Yearbook of the National Society for the Study of Education, ed. Nelson B. Henry (Chicago: NSSE, 1942), pp. 39–86.

7 The Herbartians alone, of major groups, offered an alternative to traditionalism until Dewey came long. They emphasized not the natural unfolding of the child's native gifts, as did the romantics, but formal studies or subjects without the heavy emphasis on drill, routine, and memorization tokening traditional education. Incompatible with the romantics and the traditionalists, as Krug notes, "this put them in a minority among educators of their time" (Edward A. Krug, *The Shaping of the American High School* [New York: Harper & Row, 1964], p. 99).

8 Patricia A. Graham, "Progressive Education Movement," *Encyclopedia of Education* (New York: Crowell-Collier, 1971), vol. 7, p. 249.

9 Romanticism in pedagogical theory sometimes is directly connected with authoritarian philosophic outlooks. G. Stanley Hall's theory seems a prime example of this, with its idea of "racial catharsis," whereby the child is to purge him- or herself of primitive, racial feelings. This suggests expressionism and permissiveness in child pedagogy, but it is coupled with other concepts clearly discriminatory against females and minority "races"; it is clearly supportive of an authoritarian state; and it is clearly non- (if not anti-) scientific. Hall's "child study movement" captured the fancy of many romantic progressives. The best brief account of Hall remains Merle Curti's in *The Social Ideas of American Educators* (Totowa, N.J.: Littlefield, Adams & Co., 1971), pp. 396–428.

The Freudian movement long has had its own emphasis on an expressing or "working out" of repression, which supports a type of pedagogical permissiveness. Some of the Freudians (certainly not the Freud of *Civilization and Its Discontents* and *The Future of An Illusion*, however) can be argued to have strong authoritarian leanings. See, for instance, Clarence J. Karier on Carl Jung, "The Ethics of a Therapeutic Man: C. G. Jung," *The Psychoanalytic Review* 63, no. 1 (1976): 115–46. For an excellent although brief discussion of Freudianism in connection with progressivism, see Cremin, *The Transformation of the School*, pp. 207–15.

10 Notice that this is not the same question as the one commonly raised or answered; *viz.*, "How widely did Dewey's philosophy influence American education?" Doubtless, in one way or another, he had *vast* influence—but the fact is largely insignificant. We know little about Dewey's direct influence or the direct influence of his ideas via those who followed him consistently. As a matter of fact, we are only beginning to get good, scholarly studies of some of his early pragmatic followers, such that we can analytically understand (a) how they differed from Dewey and each other, and (b) how they influenced their times. Until recently the tendency has been to think of two rather vague streams of pragmatic followers, social reconstructionists and (for want of a better label) what we might call "orthodox Deweyites," with few of the necessary critical differentiations made internally for each group. The best general work remains John L. Child's *American Pragmatism and Education* (New York: Henry Holt, 1956), one part of which is composed of chapters on Kilpatrick, Counts, and Bode. Samuel Tennenbaum's biography, *William Heard Kilpatrick*, is seriously flawed stylistically but helpful still. Especially recommended are Gerald L. Gutek's *The Educational Theory of George S. Counts* (Columbus, Ohio: The Ohio State University Press, 1970), and Peter F. Carbone, Jr., *The Social and Educational Thought of Harold Rugg* (Durham, N.C.: Duke University Press, 1977).

11 Graham, "Progressive Education Movement," p. 252.

12 To focus on teachers, even those prepared today (doubtless superior to normal school or high school graduates then) probably do not have the academic depth and breadth of understanding, and psychological expertise, Dewey calls for. About the teacher, for instance, "The practically important question concerns the conditions under which the teacher can really be the intellectual leader of a social group. The first condition goes back to his own intellectual preparation in subject matter. This should be abundant to the point of overflow. It must be much wider than the ground laid out in textbook or in any mixed plan for teaching a lesson. . . . Some of the reasons why the teacher should have an excess supply of information and understanding are too obvious to need mention. The central reason is possibly not always recognized. The teacher

must have his mind free to observe the mental responses and movements of the student members. . . . Unless the teacher's mind has mastered the subject matter in advance, unless it is thoroughly at home in it, using it unconsciously without the need of express thought, he will not be free to give full time and attention to observation and interpretation of the pupils' intellectual reactions" (John Dewey, *How We Think* [New York: D. C. Heath, 1933], pp. 274-75).

13   On the matter of how the teacher must "psychologize" the material, see John Dewey, *The Child and The Curriculum and The School and Society* (Chicago: The University of Chicago Press, 1958), pp. 19-24; idem, *How We Think*, pp. 35-68, 78-85, 260-79, 288-92; and idem, *Democracy and Education* (New York: Macmillan, 1916), pp. 212-17.

14   John Dewey and Evelyn Dewey, *Schools of Tomorrow* (New York: E. P. Dutton, 1962).

15   Dewey, *The Child and The Curriculum and The School and Society*, pp. 92-94. There are many excellent accounts of the Laboratory School, the best probably being Katherine Camp Mayhew and Anna Camp Edwards, *The Dewey School* (New York: Appleton-Century-Crofts, 1936-1964). Excellent briefer accounts are found in Melvin C. Baker, *Foundations of John Dewey's Educational Theory* (New York: King's Crown Press, 1955), pp. 136-57; and Vynce A. Hines, "Progressivism in Practice," in *A New Look at Progressive Education*, ed. James R. Squire (Washington, D.C.: Association for Supervision and Curriculum Development, 1972), pp. 118-38. The Squire volume has several discussions that invite testing of the distinctions introduced here between "pragmatic" and "romantic" progressivism.

16   John Dewey, *Experience and Education* (New York: Macmillan, 1938), p. 9.

17   From 1922; see John Dewey, *Character and Events* (New York: Henry Holt, 1929), vol. II, pp. 779-80.

18   From 1935; see John Dewey, *Problems of Men* (New York: Philosophical Library, 1946), p. 139.

19   From 1937; see ibid., p. 51.

20   From 1938; see ibid., p. 89.

21   From 1938; see ibid., pp. 42, 43-44.

22   From 1939; see John Dewey, *Freedom and Culture* (New York: Capricorn Books, 1963), pp. 149-50.

23   For the former, see John Dewey (ed. by Joseph Ratner), *Education Today* (New York: G. P. Putnam's Sons, 1940), pp. 3-17; for the latter, see *American Teacher* 12 (January 1928): 3-6. Also on teachers' need to unionize, see Dewey, *Education Today*, pp. 303-07.

24   George S. Counts, *Dare the Schools Build a New Social Order?* (New York: John Day. 1932.)

25   His idea early was that the state and society were coextensive, the former being society mainly from the governmental aspect. "Society as the real whole, is the normal order, and the mass as an aggregate of isolated units is the fiction. . . . A state represents men so far as they have become organically related to one another, or are possessed of unity of purpose or interest" (in *John Dewey: The Early Works* [Carbondale, Ill.: Southern Illinois University Press, 1969], vol. I, p. 232; also see vol. II [1967], p. 294).

26   Walter Feinberg remarks that "by dismissing prematurely a class analysis of American society in favor of the interest group theory, Dewey was unable to examine some of the structural limits to progress" ("Dewey as a Cultural Symbol: Some Reflections on Reason and Rhetoric and Its Critics," *The Gadfly* I, nos. 5 and 6 [September/October 1978], p. 16). Dewey clearly advocates class analysis, whatever might be the case about the adequacy of his dealing with structural limits to progress. Class analysis is one of three modes that he and James H. Tufts propose in *Ethics* (rev. ed. [New York: Henry Holt, 1932], p. 347-64). For his use of the concept *re* American society, see John Dewey, *Individualism Old and New* (New York: Capricorn Books, 1962), pp. 423-28; and idem, "Class Struggle and the Democratic Way," *The Social Frontier* 2 (May 1936), pp. 241-42. For his criticism of Marxism and the *Marxist* notion of class struggle (which he *does* reject), see idem, *Liberalism and Social Action* (New York: G. P. Putnam's Sons, 1935), pp. 80-93; and idem, *Freedom and Culture*, pp. 87-102.

27   Dewey, *Democracy and Education*, p. 5. Also: "At present, concentrations of industry and

division of labor have practically eliminated household and neighborhood occupations—at least for educational purposes. . . . We must recognize our compensations—the increase in toleration, in breadth of social judgment, the larger acquaintance with human nature, the sharpened alertness in reading signs of character and in interpreting social situations, greater accuracy of adaptation to differing personalities, contact with greater commercial activities" (*The Child and The Curriculum and The School and Society*, p. 12 of the latter).

28   Dewey, *The Public and Its Problems* (Denver: Alan Swallow, 1954), p. 72.

29   Ibid., p. 28.

30   Ibid., pp. 211-12. Compare this and the previous quotation to the one cited in note 25 for documentation of how the Hegelian doctrine of organic, internal relations disappeared from Dewey's thought by 1927 (when *The Public and Its Problems* was first published).

31   Hechinger's proposal seems ambiguous, to say the least. He wants a "renaissance of educational populism" that will counter the "pseudopopulists of Proposition 13," but the envisioned coalition of *his* populists "would not provide a substitute for educational reform; it would refuse any involvement with educational theories . . . " and "its mission would be limited to the propagation of faith in public schools as the foundation of American democracy." What one apparently has is the proposal of an ideology under the guise of being nonideological; a politics for education under the guise of being nonpolitical. One is reminded of the old saw, "The only bad politics is secret politics." See his "Schoolyard Blues: The Decline of Public Education," *Saturday Review*, 20 January 1979, p. 22.

32   Cremin, *The Transformation of the School*, p. 353.

33   Jo Ann Boydston and Kathleen Poulos, *Checklist of Writings about John Dewey* (Carbondale, Ill.: Southern Illinois University Press, 1978).

34   Jo Ann Boydston with Robert L. Andresen, *John Dewey: A Checklist of Translations, 1900-1967* (Carbondale, Ill.: Southern Illinois University Press, 1969).

35   The origin and earlier work of the Center was described by Jo Ann Boydston and this author in "The Dewey Project," *The Educational Forum* 35, no. 2 (January 1979): 177-83.

36   Jo Ann Boydston, ed., *Guide to the Works of John Dewey* (Carbondale, Ill.: Southern Illinois University Press, 1970).

37   See note 33, above.

38   For examples of some of the best recent anthologies of Dewey's writings: Reginald D. Archambault, ed., *John Dewey on Education: Selected Writings* (New York: Modern Library, 1964); Richard J. Bernstein, ed., *Dewey on Experience, Nature, and Freedom* (New York: Liberal Arts Press, 1960); Sidney Morgenbesser, ed., *Dewey and His Critics* (New York: The Journal of Philosophy, Inc., 1977). Some of the best recent commentaries and analyses are: Reginald D. Archambault, ed., *Dewey on Education: Appraisals* (New York: Random House, 1966); Richard J. Bernstein, *John Dewey* (New York: Washington Square Press, 1966); Steven M. Cahn, ed., *New Studies in the Philosophy of John Dewey* (Hanover, N.H.: University Press of New England, 1977); A. H. Somjee, *The Political Theory of John Dewey* (New York: Teachers College Press, 1968); and Philip M. Zeltner, *John Dewey's Aesthetic Philosophy* (Amsterdam: B. R. Gruner, 1975).

39   Carbondale, Ill.: Southern Illinois University Press, 1973. Readers interested in recent accounts of Dewey's life will also find of interest Jo Ann Boydston, ed., "Introduction," and the Dewey poems in *The Poems of John Dewey* (Carbondale, Ill.: Southern Illinois University Press, 1977); Neil Coughlain, *Young John Dewey* (Chicago: University of Chicago Press, 1975); and Charles F. Howlett, *Troubled Philosopher: John Dewey and the Struggle for World Peace* (Port Washington, N.Y.: National University Publications, 1977).

40   I venture as an example of this Israel Scheffler's *Four Pragmatists: A Critical Introduction to Peirce, James, Mead, and Dewey* (New York: Humanities Press, 1974).

41   Garry M. Brodsky, "Rescent Philosophic Work on Dewey," *The Southern Journal of Philosophy* 14, no. 3 (Fall 1976): 372.

42   So far as education is concerned, revisionism is mainly a development within the history of education, and Dewey figures as only one of several theorists about whom controversy has arisen.

For a good general discussion of this controversy within the recent history of education, see Donald R. Warren, "A Past for the Present: History, Education, and Public Philosophy," *Educational Theory* 28, no. 4 (Fall 1978): 253-65.

Walter Feinberg's *Reason and Rhetoric* (New York: John Wiley, 1975) is one of the few major works by a philosopher of education to appear in the revisionist vein. See my response to his treatment of Dewey, in "John Dewey and the Ploys of Revisionism," *Philosophical Studies in Education* (Terre Haute, Ind.: Indiana State University and The Ohio Valley Philosophy of Education Society, 1979), pp. 42-54.

43   John Dewey, *Toward a Science of Education* (New York: Horace Liveright, 1929).

44   However, a notable exception to this tendency, with a good discussion of the concept of "organism" and Dewey's educational thought, is D. C. Phillips's "John Dewey and the Organismic Archetype," in *Melbourne Studies in Education*, ed. R. J. W. Selleck (Melbourne, Australia: Melbourne University Press, 1971), pp. 232-271. Phillips does not deal with Dewey's mature political writings, where it seems most evident to this writer that Dewey carefully lets the reader know he is using the concept of organic relations is only a metaphorical sense: e.g., "What is generic and the same everywhere is at best the organic structure of man, his biological make-up. While it is evidently important to take this into account, it is also evident that none of the *distinctive* features of *human* association can be deduced from it" (*The Public and Its Problems*, p. 195). Italics are Dewey's.

45   John Dewey, *Experience and Nature*, 2nd ed. (New York: W. W. Norton & Co., 1929), p. la. Of major works to genuinely concentrate on the central role of aesthetic experience and creativity in Dewey's philosophy, I recommend George R. Geiger's *John Dewey in Perspective* (New York: Oxford University Press, 1958); and Zeltner's *Dewey's Aesthetic Theory*. Geiger, Francis T. Villemain, Hobert W. Burns, Nathanel L. Champlin, Otto Krash, Frederick C. Neff, and the author dealt with the topics from the perspective of education in "John Dewey Centennial: A Special Section," *Saturday Review*, 21 November 1959, pp. 17-26, 52.

46   John Dewey, *A Common Faith* (New Haven: Yale University Press, 1934).

47   The references generally are brief and almost of the character of "asides" as he discusses philosophy, art, science, and civilization; but I think that they consequently give one a view of religious qualities within a more synoptic and sympathetic purview than does *A Common Faith*. See, for example, John Dewey, *Quest for Certainty* (New York: Minton, Balch & Co., 1929), pp. 235ff., 276ff., 293-313; and idem, *Art As Experience*, pp. 191-95, 348-49.

Philosophy and Policy Studies: Personal Reflections

THOMAS F. GREEN
Syracuse University

More and more often nowadays, philosophers of education are actively participating in something called "policy studies." In a number of important institutions, departments of educational foundations, which include philosophers, have been reorganized (or renamed) into departments of educational or social policy. I do not know how to account for this movement in detail. It may be merely the expression of a search for relevance and survival in a period when both the education of teachers and the placement of academics reflect stronger vocational emphases than have been evident for many years. But this, no doubt, is only the most apparent feature of the scene, a feature, moreover, that reaches far beyond the scholarly enterprise within professional education.

Whatever consensus may have existed concerning the nature of liberal or general education has recently suffered erosion everywhere. Lacking that consensus, not only philosophers of education but also historians, classicists, literary scholars, and even political theorists have had to redefine and reassert their academic roles. Their established position in the scheme of things needs a fresh defense. And what more utilitarian defense is there than to incorporate such nonpractical (I do not say impractical) matters as philosophy into the study of public policy? Perhaps such realignments in academic structure are a sign of our almost childlike faith in something called virtue by association. Our relevance will be known by the friends we keep.

But why have policy studies been so favored in recent years? Again, I cannot say with any degree of certainty. But in general, and in the special case of education, it seems to have stemmed from an expanding number of actors involved in public policy. State and federal governments have entered the picture to a greater degree than before, first through funded programs attached to regulations and, later, by regulations unattached to any funding. That, in itself, would be enough to elevate the study of educational policy. But the actors, as any school superintendent knows, have also come to include parents and special publics in new ways. The President's Task Force on Youth Employment, out of a due respect for such competing interest groups, recently had to consult with more than fifty different agencies and organizations just to establish an agenda for work. Perhaps it is ironic, but nevertheless worth pondering, that the consumer protection movement has not only converted education into a prominent consumer commodity—a move, by itself, destined to distort the value of education—but also has stimulated precisely the state and federal presence that it is partly designed to counterbalance. That is to say, the result of attempts to institutionalize participatory democracy may have encouraged precisely the remote governmental management that it is intended to subvert. Then, too, in the past twenty years we have witnessed the increased presence of the courts even to the point of actually taking over the management of schools.

All this is quite obvious and well known. The effect of these developments is to elevate policy studies to a prominence they did not possess a mere fifteen or twenty years ago. Policy studies is clearly a growth industry in an age when growth in academia is hard to come by. And so it may be that whereas a few years ago philosophers of education were disposed to find their nutriment in chewing on the logic of behaviorism, they are now disposed to feed on the problems of public policy. That is where the action is. Where once they aspired to speak to leadership on problems of teaching, they now seek to give direction by attending to politics and policy.

That philosophers of education might take such a turn is understandable when viewed as the behavior of the beleagured. But is it "authorized" in any other way? Does it have other foundations? Policy decision has been described as authoritative action. What authority, then, what special skills do philosophers possess? They do not typically exercise the authority of public office. Nor is it obvious that their academic specialty bestows on them the kind of authority to speak on policy that economists, lawyers, or social scientists of some other ilk, rightly or wrongly, may claim to possess. Viewed as a practical recommendation, the idea that philosophers—as philosophers— might have some special contribution to make to public policy will no doubt come as news to most school administrators who spend many hours concerned with bargaining, buses, and budgeting. And if it is likely to strike them as odd, then how is it likely to strike your usual garden-variety legislator or school board member? Questions of educational policy do not come clearly labeled "philosophical." They are not theoretical questions. Neither are they speculative. Nor is it at all clear that if policymakers—whoever *they* are—were philosophically more astute, they would therefore make better decisions. But we should note also that to whatever extent the formation of policy is a political matter—which is a large extent indeed—then issues are likely to be decided more by the balance of interests than by the demonstration of truth. Truth is the business of philosophers, but adjusting interests is the business of politicians and managers. And, finally, to the extent that policy questions are technical—which they often are—then their formulation as well as their analysis may require technical capacities that philosophers seldom possess.

In short, there is room for a dissenting voice in this movement to subsume philosophy of education under the rubric of educational policy studies. One may doubt whether such a trend is likely to improve educational policy very much. It is, however, likely to improve educational philosophy a great deal, and that is the point in support of which I offer these decidedly personal observations.

But for a philosopher to offer his personal reflections requires some defense. Doing so smacks of an arrogance akin to a thirty-year-old seeking to present his autobiography, a genre reserved for those of elderly eminence or for those long in touch with such eminence. I can claim neither. But there is a second difficulty. Personal reflections, the record of lessons learned, has also the temper of narrative; and narrative is a mode of writing uncongenial to philosophers, except for a few truly exceptional souls. Philosophical discourse is tightly framed in argument and counterargument, and stories are not arguments. Nor do arguments make good stories. Stories may permit the reader to draw a conclusion, but they do not demand it. Arguments, on the other hand, require a conclusion. They drive the mind with inevitability and finality either to a belief or to another argument. Stories do nothing of the sort. They just point. There are times, however, when pointing may be enough.

My overarching point is that if philosophers of education become heavily engaged in the practical, muddy, and indecisive tasks of making public policy, then they are likely to learn a great deal that is philosophically useful; and the philosophical import of what they learn is likely to exceed by far the worth of their contributions to the formation of policy. I advance this view as no more than a personal belief, and I do not pretend to offer as evidence any more than my own experience.

Some years ago, as part of my own education in management and public policy, I took leave from my university position and accepted employment with a land developer committed to creating a New Town in the neighborhood of Rochester, New York. My responsibilities were to provide leadership in planning and developing a new school district that would be coextensive with the zoned boundaries of the New Town development. Within those boundaries there were no existing school buildings. The problem was to create a new authority, design new buildings, determine their finance and their placement in the land development sequence, and determine answers to these problems in the light of a basic approach to education for all age groups within the future community. It was an extraordinary opportunity to become involved in every aspect of educational planning from the formulation of basic philosophy to the design, finance, construction, and staffing of schools. Sooner or later in such an enterprise, every significant question of educational policy from state and local government and the day-to-day management of schools to all the problems of long-range planning must appear.

The developer wished to approach the problems of education within a set of highly innovative objectives. He was concerned to lower the capital costs of school construction first by eliminating duplication of facilities in the community and second by producing complex revenue sources for all public facilities. Athletic fields and recreational facilities, for example, would be constructed so as to be used by schools for educational programs but also by a variety of community groups on a time-lease basis. If the school included an auditorium, then it would be designed so as to be available for lease as a local cinema operated for profit or as a facility for lease to community groups for theater productions. The swimming pool was to be constructed so that it could be leased by associations of residents and would adjoin a fast-food delivery station that in the summer could be operated as a business and during the school year could be used to provide subsidized meals for school lunches.

In short, it was supposed that by creating many such public facilities with associated entrepreneurial opportunities, the sources of capital funds would be multiplied and residents would benefit by lower taxes for bonding public facilities. But in order to do this, all public facilities from the golf course and the marina to greenhouses associated with schools, parks, art galleries, and centers for vocational education would be owned by a separate Public Facilities Corporation. The schools, in short, would never be owned by the school board of the local district. Instead, the school board would be free to lease facilities as they were needed, for as much time as they were needed, at whatever locations they were needed, and with shared costs of maintenance and debt service.

This is an ingenious concept. It represents an alternative approach to the creation of public facilities. Given quite reasonable estimates of population growth, levels of tax revenues, state aid of various sorts, and existing experience in already developed New Towns, we anticipated that the tax savings to the residents could run as high as 40 percent compared with what they would otherwise pay. That is a substantial difference. But though the anticipated gains were interestingly large, the difficulties were larger and even more interesting.

Can the state pay capital aid to a school district that does not have title to its facilities? What does capital aid *mean* under conditions where the school board is engaged only in leasing facilities? How is it possible to write a lease in which not only are the costs of amortization, including debt service and maintenance, distributed over a period of years, but in which revenues are calculated on a daily or hourly basis per square foot of space used? In a building used by the schools *and* by other groups as well, who owns what part of the permanent fixtures? Can we sustain the legal fiction of a nonprofit corporation that owns extensive property including commercial leases and at the same time preserve its tax-exempt status? If that cannot be done, then even if such a corporation had bonding power, and even if it could receive state capital aid, its bonds would become like commercial bonds, the interest rates would have to be correspondingly higher to attract investors, and the benefits to the taxpayer would be lost.

As I studied such questions in minute detail, two problems that before I had entertained only theoretically began to impress themselves more forcefully on my consciousness. The first was that as we struggled to bring the facilities corporation into existence, the distinction between public and private enterprise increasingly assumed the status of a hard and basic reality. I began to discover, in short, just how fundamentally our legal definitions of property reinforce the assumptions of private enterprise and place limitations on the employment of social imagination. I learned all over again what my teachers had said for years—that philosophical theory is not *merely* theory. It is not "strictly academic." It describes, in fact, the most basic realities of our social system.

The second was the discovery in these planning problems of a context within which one could actually arrive at carefully reasoned conclusions on an entire series of large public questions. For example, planning provided a real context within which to consider whether interest from municipal bonds should be tax-exempt. One could transform this question from its typical rendering as a matter of principle into hard estimates of the costs to citizens in both taxes and diminished public facilities if such interest were no longer exempt from income taxes. I discovered that a line of action I was morally disposed to support carried with it substantial social costs to myself, to my children, and to my neighbors. In short, both the philosophical relevance and the social reality of such questions were impressed on me with a force I had not known before. Philosophy took on a fresh vitality! Solving a series of practical problems turned out to be philosophically informative.

But once we start down this path of planning and reflection, other questions of importance arise. Would it be possible to use state funds, currently provided for busing, in order to subsidize a municipal transportation system also owned and operated by a facilities corporation? Could the school board lease facilities constructed as residences and use them for early childhood centers and for elementary instruction through the first three grades so that capital costs would be totally recovered by the eventual sale of those facilities as homes? Can the Federal Housing Administration (FHA) finance schools? But assuming that this can be done, then how many such centers will be needed? What is the best medical judgment as to how far youngsters of differing ages should be expected to walk to school? Can we anticipate the likely movement of the population in the first and second decades of development so as to optimize the low cost and local availability of educational resources? Should the school system include a middle school? If not, then why not? What grade arrangement is educationally best and what arrangement is most likely to be both educationally sound and also attractive for marketing? Could we have a system that is not age-graded? One that mixes the generations? How?

In every school district in America answers to these questions are given even though the questions themselves are not often asked. But to confront them all at once can be intellectually immobilizing. It can also be a stunning kind of holistic lesson in what educational policy is and how it is related to government, finance, transportation, the long-term future, the economy, and to conflicting views about how education should be carried out. Yet, why should we suppose that philosophers have any expertise in handling such problems? These are questions that sound like those asked by students of business, public administration, management, or political science—but not philosophy or psychology.

Nevertheless, there are substantial lessons to be learned, even about philosophy of education, by attempting to deal with such questions. I list them in no particular order and with no thesis about their internal connection.

First, it is worth noting that immersion in the academic disciplines does have differential effects on the kinds of intellectual and moral virtues that persons develop. One of the problems for a philosopher engaging in policy formation is that, in such work, for the most part details possess a *visibly* heavy weight and philosophical principles do not. The virtues of the philosopher are those needed to always seek and formulate the general principle, the normative guide to conduct, that underlies the murky details of daily life. But the business of planning is the day-to-day accumulation of data, their analysis, and their array for quick communication on decisions pending; and in that effort it is difficult for overall humane objectives to retain even the most fragile visibility. Philosophically endorsed principles may be the distillate of such work, but they are not its point.

Philosophers, furthermore, demand the tenacity needed to drive to the completion of an argument. Omissions are disturbing. Counter-arguments cannot be ignored. Philosophers require parsimony in method, but are unlikely to purchase it at the cost of thoroughness. They are likely, like scientists, to resist judgment until the data are in or, unlike scientists, to ignore the data altogether as a distraction. But in the affairs of policy analysis and policy decision the data cannot be ignored, and they are never in. The argument is never complete. Judgment based on crude data inelegantly developed but arriving on time is better than refined information leading to knowledge, but arriving too late. In policy formation we seek the momentary grasp of things that will permit judgment; in philosophy we seek the durable formula that can be called knowledge.

All this is enough to make philosophers understandably nervous and uncomfortable. None of it is their long suit. For example, I had the experience of responding within a ten-day period to management's request for a memorandum setting forth their own school tax burden over a long period of time and advising them whether and *with what marginal effect* it might be helpful to make a cash donation to the school board so as to create an initial positive cash flow for the district. The question was important for three reasons—first, because being nearly the sole property owner in such an enterprise, the developer is the principal taxpayer for schools; second, because it is difficult to sell houses where taxes are high; and third, because since the district had no cash flow with which to begin the first year, initial tax rates would probably be very high.

In composing such a memo one learns quickly—in a matter of days—how the cash flow of state aid and local tax collections influences the decisions of local districts and whether any attempt to prefinance education would alter the immediate tax burden of the developer, his own cash flow, and the long-term tax burden of future residents, and how it would affect the educational programs that could be provided for children.

One could view this as a rather typical problem of management. And that would be correct. But it is also a problem of policy, or the analysis of policy or the effects of existing policy. In any case, it is not a problem of philosophy. I discovered that though I could quickly learn to do the task, it was harder for me and required more intense concentration than was needed by others more experienced in finance and business management. I was learning to appreciate and to some extent cultivate the intellectual virtues that these others possessed by virtue of their training. But it did not occur to me that my own philosophical education gave me any advantage. On the contrary, such sensibilities and marks of temperament, more often than not, seemed to be liabilities. I found myself shockingly prepared either to unlearn those virtues or to set them aside, and to abandon my identity as a philosopher. I found myself also delighted to acquire a new respect for the skills and intellectual virtues of the competent manager and planner. Their own virtues seemed to me often more creative, equally as demanding, and frequently as personally rewarding in their exercise as the intellectual virtues of the philosopher. Their activities, I came to believe, were rigorously disciplined, but philosophy was not the name of the discipline. Nonetheless, the experience remains for me an important lesson in the philosophy of curriculum.

But it had more meaning than that. I became more and more convinced that if you want to understand the metaphysics of society, those intractable necessities of structure, form, and movement that describe the way things work, then do not forsake the skills of the accountant; and if you care to learn how social values are actually created and distributed, then immerse yourself in the necessities of actually deciding on questions of taxation, public finance, and the political as well as technical details of public budgeting. The accountant has control of one way to describe the humanly important flow of goods in our society; and the process of budgeting, despite its difficult ambiguities, is one way we actually influence the distribution of the arts, learning, work, and education. These are not the only ways, but they are important and fundamental, and they are, to a large extent, the ways of public policy.

There is in all this a double problem. On the one hand it illuminates the subject matter of philosophy and on the other poses the most serious questions about the proper education of leaders. I believe it is true that persons in economics, public finance, and accounting have in hand the tools needed to understand the formation of public policy. But I also think that they tend to apply such tools too narrowly. Their employment of them is often impoverished. Accountants, for example, have the means at hand, but do not turn with imagination to formulate the social balance sheet for such goods as security and justice, health and hope and the elevation of culture. They could, but they do not. That is not their special virtue. Philosophers, on the other hand, are likely to see the point and desirability of finding new ways of speaking of cost and benefit, but they are unlikely to master the skills needed to actually do it. At the same time the technicians of public policy are likely to see the necessity of their skills and to magnify the difficulty in extending their application Why can we not get both rational argument, of the sort that philosophers know, and at the same time skillful action of the sort that good public leaders often display? That, it seems to me, is a serious and important question in the philosophy of education, a problem in the education of citizens.

But allow me to attack the point directly. I doubt very much that public accounting and budgeting will be improved by the contributions of philosophers. But I come to the view that in these disciplines of management and public policy a philosopher can discover an extension of moral and social philosophy. The activities of public policy—its formation, promulgation, management, and amendment—are the practical ways in which we give worldly expression to our understanding of good and evil, our care for neighbor, and our understanding of what constitutes a good society. Legislation, budgeting, and administration, seen in this light, are the practices whose corresponding theory is the theory of good and evil and of social value. And mastering the skills of public policy can be the means of conducting an extensive inquiry into the metaphysics of modern society.

The point is not, therefore, that philosophers of education can contribute to the formation of public policy. They are no more likely to do so than historians or plumbers or any other disciplined body of citizens. The point is rather that engaging in such activities is a good way—not the only way—of actually discovering what philosophy of education is about. It is one way of gathering the data, the concrete material, that a philosopher can use for reflection. If it produces better philosophy, that can be rewarding even if it does not improve policy.

But there are other lessons that have seemed to me important. I have become increasingly and reluctantly persuaded that decisions of educational policy are practically never decided on grounds of educational theory. Several years ago one could easily gain the impression from the prevailing design of elementary school buildings in New York State that the theory of open education was being adopted everywhere. It seemed on the edge of becoming "official policy," a significant victory for educational theory. But a deeper look would quickly reveal that the state formula for capital aid to local districts was based on the pupil-rated capacity of the proposed structure, and that hallways did not count. So anyone who could build a structure without hallways—a design that tended to look like the adoption of open education—would receive a greater share of capital aid. That is a highly attractive result to local taxpayers in any neighborhood. It does not represent any widespread decision to adopt a particular educational argument. We would have had a clear victory of educational theory only if such designs had been adopted despite their *greater* local cost.

In 1980–1981, the basic federal legislation on vocational education will come up for reauthorization in the Congress. This is legislation originally proposed to provide matching funds—one state dollar for each federal dollar. Currently, however, no state raises less than six dollars for each federal dollar. The original intention was to stimulate the states to adopt a federal policy. They have done so. The policy question therefore becomes: Why should the federal government continue a policy that has already succeeded and has been adopted by the states? This question remains *no matter how educationally beneficial or successful such programs are.* If the policy is continued— as it probably will be—the decision is unlikely to have been made on educational grounds.

In general, if an argument of educational theory is to prevail in the policy debate, it will have to meet two conditions simultaneously. First of all, the argument will have to be conclusive. That is to say, it must be decisive. But it must also be decisive in promoting a difference of substantial magnitude. In short, it will have to be a strong argument and a substantial one. There are very few arguments of this sort arising either from educational theory or from educational research. Understand! I am not saying that educational arguments are never useful. I am suggesting rather that they are almost never decisive in policy decisions, and that they are likely to be used only when they reinforce decisions for which there is already some other acceptable argument

constitute a substantial philosophical account of the nature of
.nd evil and the virtues required by the good life. Such a study
have to include a sensitive account of that peculiar alchemy by
good is transformed into evil and evil into good. It would
.ute a major topic of moral education, but one that, in the
e of any participation in public affairs, philosophers are
.ly to attempt or, attempting, are unlikely to do very well. Yet it is
al problem for educational philosophy.

study of public policy is the study of public virtue and its spread,
. the community and in its leaders. I have come to the conclusion
.rticipation in the formation of public policy is the practice
.heory is the theory of good and evil. The formation and spread
.e and the nature of good and evil are and always have been
problems in the philosophical tradition. They become serious
.ns for the philosophy of education. We do not, or should not,
.her the pleasures or the benefits of philosophy through its
.tion to this or that field of human work. We should not seek to
philosophy" to public policy.
.sophy is not a body of knowledge that can be mastered and,
.nastered, then applied as if it provided formulae for other
activities. It is rather the expression of an intractable human
understand the deeper character of our lives and the activities
.ves include. But, by the same token, such reflections are
. to be much good, they are unlikely to illumine the problems
.n beings, unless philosophers also engage in those activities.
.he current movement of philosophers into something called
.tudies, even if undertaken to establish some relevance to the
.f the world, is likely to remain as unrelated and as irrelevant as
.nless philosophers come to be actually engaged in the murky
of policy formation. In doing so, they may contribute little to
.ovement of policy, but their doing so is likely to contribute a
.al to the improvement of philosophy. Such is my own
.ce and my own conviction.

advanced on quite other grounds. Again, this is a result likely to be
unnerving to a philosopher of education who aims to offer effective
criticism of policy or to make an effective contribution. Researchers
often complain that their work is ignored by policymakers, and they
are right. Philosophers, even those working in departments of
educational policy studies, are likely to find the same thing.

But this reference to policymakers points to still another matter of
philosophical importance. If by policymakers is meant some group of
persons who, by taking counsel and by considering what is morally
best or socially desirable, can decide on what to do and implement it,
then there is no such clearly defined group in America. The word
policymakers, understood in this way, refers to the null class.

For example, no one familiar with the apparatus for educational
policy in the state of New Jersey could suppose that the highest legal
educational official in the state, the commissioner, is able to make
policy to any extent approaching what he would probably prefer. In
that state there are three different legislative committees on education.
In addition, there is a thorough bureaucratic division between
elementary and secondary education, on the one hand, and higher
education, on the other. There are also agencies outside the state
education department legally responsible for important aspects of
educational policy. Then, too, one must consider the power of local
political machines that can decisively determine state policy even in
ways contradictory to what is preferred in the state department of
education. Finally, there is the New Jersey Education Association, a
powerful organization that in some areas has greater technical
resources than can be assembled by the state itself. Things are often
other than what they seem.

Under such circumstances, the best that anyone can attempt,
including the state's highest educational official, is to influence the
ultimate course of these different forces. And there will be many, rather
than few, who will attempt to do that. The commissioner of education
in New Jersey probably has greater legally defined powers than the
commissioner in any other state. Yet his office can by no means be
pointed to as the locus of educational policy. This is a situation not
unique to New Jersey. It is the same in other states, in the federal
government, and in other institutions where educational policy is
often supposed to be established.

Again, two quite old-fashioned lessons of political philosophy
emerge. In the social enterprise called education, something like
baronial fiefdoms from time to time arise. But they are not long-lived.

In any case, there are no kings and queens, no bodies who by edict can make their will, their sense of good and bad prevail. I have the impression—perhaps mistakenly—that many academics tend to see this state of affairs as defect. I tend to see it as virtue. They, like many bureaucrats, see it as evidence of governmental failure, an incapacity to do what the common good requires, a failure of will, a disarray of authority. And in parallel fashion I have the impression that when academics speak of policy studies they have in mind not contributing to the policy process, but trying to rationally determine what is the best thing that policymakers ought to have done. The trouble is that what rationality, or even good scholarship—to say nothing of philosophy— may determine to be the best thing to do often turns out not to be doable, and, in the long run, often not to have been desirable anyway.

If we had kings and queens and strong baronial enclaves of power and authority in education, then things would no doubt be more rationalized. The locus of educational policy would be clearer and responsibility for change more focused. But in the process of purchasing clarity, we would have altered our political order so as to pay a devastating cost in the preservation of free institutions.

It is worth remembering that in no well-developed social utopia is there ever anything resembling politics. In utopia, politics is always transformed into administration and management. And the reason is that the point of such utopian visions is always to establish that predetermined balance of elemental goods that human welfare demands. Whatever remains to be done must prohibit any alteration in that predetermined balance. What remains can only be its maintenance. In contrast, it is part of the genius of our political institutions that we do not admit that anyone possesses so much wisdom as to know the appropriate balance of all the conflicting goods that we require. Least of all is it likely that "the managers" will have such wisdom. It is a good thing, in short, that there are no kings of education. But if there are none, then neither are there philosopher kings. Politics is what we cannot do without. Perhaps it is true that in educational policy the presiding rule should not be to do as much good as we can imagine, but to do as little harm as we can manage.

I venture the surmise that philosophers who became heavily engaged in the formation of educational policy will find their philosophy transformed and its vital connection to the deeper lives of persons renewed. At least I believe that I have found it so. In my own reflections I can detect a subtle shift of interest away from the problems of *policy* to the problems that any *person* will have to confront if he is

to participate in their resolution. Some o
often disposed to view such persons a
uneducated, seduced by power that they d
least naive and inept. And, indeed, there a
of bureaucrats, legislators, and public ser
persons among academics. What impres
more in both groups. It seems to me a mat
importance to seriously consider and to ex
intellectual and moral virtues that are d
affairs.

How, for example, can a public lea
absence of privacy, with the fact that
responsibility often lends a presumption
observations and speculations about wh
that problem? What moral resources are
with the temporality of policy position
excessively long hours of hard work, ne
can be undone and even one's livelihood
How does one retain a sense of patienc
large failure after long effort and the a
change in the policy process? How ca
accommodate the fact that justice may
of efficiency? If policy leaders found it
adjust their conduct as academics do, th
"throw the rascals out" almost on a we
deeper value of elections? What moral
deal with time, with the need to *do* wha
now, but benefit them later, or what m
disastrous in the long run? Can anyon
of good and evil? Can anyone in a poli
And even if such knowledge is possib
hinder a person in a policy position?
need to do bad things at the moment o
worse and doing nothing would be i

These are not artificial question
conversations I have had with pers
educational policy. They are, how
attention from the technical issues of
of character that define participatio
that the peculiar mixture of intellect
exemplified by public leaders and re

Philosophy of Education for Educators: The Eightieth NSSE Yearbook

JONAS F. SOLTIS
Teachers College, Columbia University

Aristotle has said, "Philosophy begins in wonder," but sometimes it seems that wonder may lead us away from rather than toward philosophy. I suspect that many educators have had reason to wonder what has happened to philosophy of education since mid-century. Where are the passionate debates between progressives and traditionalists, pragmatists and idealists, or between any philosophical factions warring over what education is really about? Where are the bold statements of aims and purposes, the comprehensive views of education in a democratic society, the vision and inspiration dedicated educators need? Have philosophers really just come to play with words or with their existential selves? Can they speak to each other only in a technical language incomprehensible to the practicing professional? Does philosophy have *anything* of worth to offer educators?

These and a host of similar questions are in need of answers if the field of philosophy of education is to have renewed meaning for educators today. But how do you display the relevant goings-on in a scholarly field like philosophy of education in 1980 when: (1) there is no agreement among its scholars on how the field should be descriptively ordered; (2) there is no dominant philosophy nor single acceptable paradigm in the field; (3) like all other scholarly fields in the twentieth century, philosophy has grown more technical; and (4) people expect from philosophers something different from what they ordinarily get? These were the problems confronting the designer, editorial committee, and authors of the eightieth National Society for the Study of Education (NSSE) yearbook with its focus on philosophy of education. This article describes the framework and contents of that forthcoming volume, tries to right wrong expectations of what philosophers have to offer educators, describes the proper role of philosophy in the education of educators, and outlines a curriculum for doctoral programs in philosophy of education.[1]

I

The key to finding a suitable structure for the eightieth yearbook was the recognition of a serious professional mismatch between expectation and delivery. The philosophical expectations of professional educators were not being met by what was being delivered by professional philosophers of education. For many people, *philosophy* means "a way of life" and correspondingly, for many educators, philosophy of education means "a way of educating." This is a very sensible and useful meaning of the term *philosophy*, but it is not the only one nor does it reflect very accurately what professional philosophers have been about since mid-century.[2] It does, however, nicely reflect the form of the very influential earlier Brubacher NSSE yearbooks of 1942 and 1955, with their "schools of philosophy" structure, which in turn reflected the way professional philosophers structured the field at that time. A systematic way of looking at the world and life was applied to the conceptualization of a way of educating, and for many educators trained since World War II this was their singular exposure to philosophy of education. Making sense of the whole and developing a consistent set of values, beliefs, and goals is still a highly desirable enterprise for educators, but it is not the only way educators can be philosophical or make practical use of philosophy.

To demonstrate the shift in philosophical work between yearbooks and how educators can also use philosophy, the distinction between the noun *philosophy* and the verb *philosophize* is helpful. In the noun sense, philosophy is a thing, a product of philosophical thinking like the philosophy of Dewey or of Marx or like pragmatism, Thomism, or existentialism. The verb philosophize comprises a set of activities of elucidation, argument, critique, clarification, analysis, synthesis, and so forth, aimed at reflecting on how we think about the world and our actions in it.

In recent years, philosophers of education, like philosophers in general, have been less inclined to build or interpret systems of philosophy and have been more engaged in examining a number of topics and ideas relevant to educating by the use of their highly honed philosophical skills. Thus they have tended to view philosophy less as a noun and more as a verb, less as system building and more as ways of thinking critically about some important aspect of educating, like teaching competency, equality of educational opportunity, the nature of educational research, and so forth. They have tried to use philosophy to help educators to think more clearly about what they are doing. Through the activity of doing philosophy, they provide elucidations, reflections, critical appraisals, and conceptual frameworks for ordering ideas, analyzing educational situations, considering options, designing curricula, making judgments, and in general understanding what the many bits and pieces of the complex educational enterprise are about. Clearly, if an educator is looking for a comprehensive view of education, a philosophical discussion dealing only with the idea of equal educational opportunity, say, no matter how cogent, would fall short of the mark as would even a collection of such philosophical papers on various topics. The many parts are always less than the whole.

But if this reflects the current state of the field, and I believe it does, then what does this say to the structuring of a yearbook and righting the misexpectations of educators? One could pick a representative group of educational philosophers, let them go at it, and alphabetize the result by author or title or find some equally arbitrary way to put the resulting set of chapters between covers. Such a solution might lead educators to expect that in philosophy of education anything goes (and indeed, it does!). But that seemed not to be a very satisfying solution to the problem. It would give no indication of where philosophers draw their strategies, arguments, concepts, theories, principles, category systems, and so forth, from, nor would it provide an easily grasped structure for nonphilosophers to use to order and reset their expectations in a meaningful way.

The solution to this problem, which now seems simple and obvious, took some time to emerge from among competing solutions offered to the NSSE Board of Directors and, if I know my philosophical colleagues, it will prove to be a debatable and philosophically inadequate solution for many of them. Still, it has had these important characteristics: It provides a simple, understandable order; it is comprehensive; and it has the flexibility to adapt to changes and new concerns inevitably to be found in both philosophy and education in the near future. The basic idea for the solution is drawn from one of the ways in which philosophy in general is ordered in colleges and universities today, by means of its subfields of philosophical inquiry like ethics, logic, aesthetics; philosophy of science, of history, of language, and so forth. Each of these subareas has a special literature, a set of concepts, arguments, theories, major figures, and philosophical problems that provide a rich context for locating and dealing with important philosophical and (for our purposes) educational issues, topics, or ideas, Moreover, as philosophical, societal, and educational winds shift, certain subareas of philosophy become temporarily more relevant to the elucidation of some equally opportune educational topic, as attested by the recent heightened interest in such subfields and topics as philosophy of science, educational research, ethics and moral education, philosophical psychology, and Piagetian views of development.

The major advantage of adopting a structure for the yearbook based on a subarea of philosophical inquiry schema is to set the reader to expect something less global than *a* philosophy of education and to focus attention on some particular dimension of education, for example, the moral, the social, the aesthetic, the epistemological. The positive aspect of this focusing is more important than the extinction of the more general expectation. An educator deeply concerned about principles of social justice and equity in education migh. hope to find them dealt with in a literature of social philosophy and education but surely would not expect their treatment in a chapter or book on philosophy of science and educational research, nor would a general work on philosophy of education necessarily include that topic. Thus, the subareas-of-philosophy structure provides for a better match of expectation and philosophical delivery with this narrower labeling of the philosophical focus and context.

Clearly, it would have been impossible to treat every subarea of philosophy in the yearbook and the major subareas of aesthetics, ethics, epistemology, logic, social philosophy, and metaphysics were chosen because they form a basic and comprehensive division of philosophy in general. The subarea of philosophy of science was also included because of the recent strong interest in it among both philosophers and educational researchers. One other accommodation to the subarea framework had to be made to reflect the fact that philosophy of education is itself a subarea of philosophy. As such, there is a part of it that focuses philosophical inquiry directly on the unique aspects of education as a human institution and phenomenon in its own right and produces theories about such things as curriculum and teaching per se. Just as a literature has grown up regarding concepts of scientific method in philosophy of science and theories of art in aesthetics, so philosophers of education have developed a literature of curricular and pedagogical theory. Thus, two chapters, one on each of these topics, were included in the yearbook. The content of the yearbook can now be briefly described.

II

After a preface that describes the structure of the yearbook, much as was done here, there is an introductory chapter by Harry S. Broudy, distinguished professor emeritus of the University of Illinois, sketch-ing directions taken by philosophy of education between yearbooks, from which the lead article in this special issue is derived. Jane R. Martin of the University of Massachusetts–Boston and president-elect of the Philosophy of Education Society follows with a chapter that takes curriculum theory as its philosophical context and focuses on the persistent Western idea of a liberal education. Reflecting on this educational ideal in our tradition, she argues that the received con-temporary view of philosophical curriculum theorists as exemplified by the work of the British philosopher Paul Hirst is dangerously narrow even though it does reflect one dominant view of liberal education as the development of the mind via the achievement of disciplined knowledge. Granting the importance of acquiring such knowledge, she wonders if this view of liberal education might not be too narrow and tend to produce the ivory tower person

> who can reason, but who has no desire to solve real problems in the real world; one who understands science, but does not worry about the uses to which it's put; one who grasps the concepts of biology, but is not disposed to exercise or to eat wisely; one who can reach flawless moral conclusions, but has neither the sensitivity nor the skill to carry them out effectively.[3]

She believes that it will do no good today to argue that possession of such knowledge will result in the development of competent, sensitive and liberally educated members of society. Perhaps,

> in a society whose dominant institutions fostered virtues such as caring about others, a sense of justice, honesty, and benevolent action, faith in the sufficiency of an initiation into the forms of knowledge might be justified. . . . [But] in a society whose institutions encourage conformity of thought and action, a desire for instant riches and worship of self—that is in our society—such faith is nothing but a pious dream.

Therefore, it should be apparent that elaborate analyses of the nature of knowledge, of its forms and of its structure, will not produce an adequate view of the curriculum content or objectives of a liberal education. To believe that it can is to commit the "epistemological fallacy," invalidly arguing from the nature of knowledge to what ought to be learned.

> In choosing curricular content and objectives we must make value judgments about our educational purposes and we set these, in turn, in relation to the moral, social, and political order we believe to be desirable. . . . The epistemological fallacy encourages philosophers and

educators to take the structure of knowledge and run. It fosters the illusion that curriculum can be determined without their asking questions about the good life and good society. Nothing could be further from the truth.

Dr. Martin ends her chapter with a sketch of the directions she sees as viable for addressing the problem of guiding the vision of those who would liberally educate. She advocates a broader view of education as the development of persons, individuals who must be seen not only as autonomous beings but also as integral parts of both the social and natural worlds.

Donna H. Kerr, professor of philosophy and education at the University of Washington, Seattle, takes up the problem of judging quality in teaching in her chapter on theory of teaching. She argues that for all our efforts as philosophers and educational theorists, programs of educational research, teacher education, and the evaluation of teaching still lack an adequate theoretical description of teaching. She cites five reasons for this deficiency: the mistaken belief that theory of teaching is reducible to theory of learning; the misconstrual of theories of phenomena related to teaching as theory of teaching itself; the confounding of theory of empirical phenomena with theory of practice; the erroneous view of theory and practice as dichotomous; and the false belief that the development of theory of teaching is either logically impossible or useless.

She seeks an answer in the construction of a general theory of teaching *as a theory of practice* that can provide the basis for judging quality in teaching. Pointing out the limitations of metaphorical language for theory development and noting that behavioral language omits reference to persons as purposeful agents and restricts evaluations of teaching to efficacy considerations, she justifies her choice of using "action language" because "it enables us to label events as *teaching* events if they are in some way part of what someone is doing *to the end* of helping someone learn something." She argues that teaching is teaching precisely because someone has selected something to be learned, has designed a plan to help bring that learning about, and has acted on the plan, and that we should be able to judge the quality of such selection, design, and action. While this is a theoretical description of teaching, its point is not like that of a theory of natural phenomena, that is, "to improve our understanding of those phenomena for purposes of prediction; the point of a theory of practice is to augment our understanding of that practice for purposes of improving the actions that constitute the practice."

Kerr identifies the following as pedagogically relevant considerations in judging quality in teaching:

> First, from the understanding of teaching as actions intended to encourage
> *persons* to *learn* things, we see that the nature of subject matter to be
> learned, the nature of learning, the nature of the particular learner or
> learners, and the nature of available means and resources for encouraging
> persons to learn particular things constitute part of the relevant con-
> siderations of teaching actions. Second, since to encourage persons to learn
> particular things is to "intervene" in the lives of others and to promote
> particular values, understandings, appreciations, etc., that are supportive
> of particular ways of living and interacting, teaching actions are inexorably
> political and moral in nature. Thus, the political and moral contexts are
> also relevant considerations of teaching actions, and third, [since] any one
> component teaching action (whether selecting . . . , designing . . . , or
> acting on the plan to encourage that learning) takes place within the
> context of the two other component teaching actions, [their relationship to
> each other is a relevant consideration].

Teachers' choices in each of these dimensions can be judged with
respect to the teacher's own ability to bring relevant beliefs and values
to bear in his or her teaching actions and on the adequacy of the
teacher's selection, design, and actions as judged from the point of view
of the relevant beliefs and values of the appropriate knowledge
community and the given moral and political context.

She ends her chapter with this argument:

> Until we develop a proper theory of teaching [that takes such aspects of
> human agency in teaching into account], we will fail to understand what
> consitutes excellence in teaching. Until then, our attempts to evaluate
> teaching will be wide of the mark. Until then, our empirical research
> presently focused on "teaching effectiveness" will fail to regard the quality
> of teaching. Until then, we shall not understand teaching well enough to
> practice it, much less to teach it, that is, until we attend to the quality of
> relevant beliefs and values brought to bear in teaching, we shall
> misunderstand the practice of teaching and so miscast our inquiries.

My own chapter, which is based on my William Heard Kilpatrick
inaugural lecture and written from the perspective of epistemology,
surveys a number of contemporary views of knowledge on the premise
that how educators conceive of knowledge will greatly affect how and
what they do as transmitters of knowledge. If we view knowledge as
embedded in words, then we tend to neglect skill acquisition and
social-personal development. If we view knowledge as relative, then we
tend to treat every opinion as equal to any other and give students the

sense that there is no sound basis for making warranted claims to know something. If we treat knowledge as theoretical and abstract, then we see none but an esoteric connection between learning and the everyday business of living, thus perpetuating the separation of school from life.

Noting that contemporary theorists of even very different persuasions have come to recognize that knowledge cannot be separated from the knower, that human beings construct different knowledge systems, and that all knowledge is embedded in the fabric of social life, the question "To what do such views necessarily commit us as educators?" is pursued in different forms. On the one hand, it is conceded that acknowledging the personal and social dimensions of knowledge forces a modification of a purely objectivist view of knowledge, while on the other, such acknowledgement adds to our sense of knowledge as an active, developing, human means of dealing with the world both individually and collectively.

If we acknowledge that our culture, our language, and our society transmit invisible messages and values, this does not mean that we cannot make them visible, that we should not transmit them to our students, or that we cannot radically critique and even alter the received system. If, for example, we judge the unconscious transmission of appropriate sex-role behavior to be detrimental to what we also judge to be an important social concern, for example, women's rights, then we can act to eliminate, modify, or equalize sex-role information transmitted by school materials and personnel as indeed educators have done.

An examination is made of the view that different forms of knowledge reflect the fact that different kinds of human experience require different ways of justifying a claim to know something. In art, for instance, beauty is judged on different grounds from those the scientist uses for empirical truth and judges use for justice. Recognition of different methods or ways of knowing and different standards for making judgments and separation of method from content in a subject matter field provide valuable perspective for the educator who would teach students to make reasonable claims. It is also argued that while the existence of different paradigms, conceptual frameworks, or ways of seeing the world do present serious difficulties in communication and understanding, they do not present insuperable obstacles to the educator who is sensitive to characteristics like ethnic group, social class, developmental stage, genetic endowment, and the idiosyncratic personal background of students. The essay ends urging that educators make wise use of these many contemporary insights into the nature of knowledge to guide sound educational practice.

Writing from the perspective of aesthetics, Maxine Greene, William F. Russell Professor in the foundations of education at Teachers College, Columbia University, argues that the aesthetic mode of human understanding ought to be given a central place among the other forms of knowledge in the curriculum. "Few educators," she observes "consider the possibility that the capacities needed for grasping and enjoying diverse works of art may be as basic as those required for verbal and numerical literacy." Her chapter is directed at giving educational meaning to the idea of "aesthetic literacy." First she distinguishes aesthetic literacy from art appreciation, the former being a more basic and general capacity to fully experience the aesthetic and the latter an ability to use the particular structures and standards of individual art forms. Then she goes on to more fully explicate the idea of aesthetic literacy as it integrates the perceptual, the emotional, the imaginative, and the cognitive into a single yet complete "province of meaning" and form of human awareness.

She takes cognizance of the various perspectives provided in philosophical aesthetics on conceptions of art and draws upon her rich reservoir of knowledge of the arts to illustrate how teachers might aid students in the acquisition of aesthetic literacy.

> To use the term literacy in this connection is to suggest that there are certain decoding or interpretive skills, certain modes of "knowing how" involved in fully realized encounters with the arts. It is also to suggest that the discrimination, sensitivity, and responsiveness made possible by such literacy contribute to understanding of the world around us. No form of literacy is sought for its own sake. Like verbal and numerical literacy, aesthetic literacy provides acquaintance with specifiable languages, as it does with particular ways of perceiving and imagining. All these are modes of extending acquaintance with the appearance of things, as they are modes of enlarging the symbolic repertoires needed for thinking about the world and expressing what is thought. . . . And aesthetic literacy is like any other mode of literacy: it can and should be taught.

She argues that this broad view of the aesthetic domain makes it impossible to view the arts as ornamental, as therapeutic, or as frills, and that it would be wrong to leave the training in aesthetic literacy to arts specialists only. The human capacity to achieve awareness of the aesthetic domain is pervasive and each teacher can and should cultivate this capacity to find meaning in a basic dimension of human life.

Professor Robert H. Ennis of the University of Illinois brings to bear his many years of work in logic as he presents a detailed conception of rational thinking and urges its incorporation into the goals of education as well as into such educational practices as teaching, evaluation, policy determination, research, and administration. He argues that we need a detailed characterization of rational thinking as it is applied in everyday life if we are to be able to formulate effective ways of teaching and using it as educators. Such a view of rational thinking needs also to go beyond aspects of formal logic and include creative, valuational, and attitudinal features of the practical and rational thinker in action.

Ennis outlines his extensive description and uses the major part of his essay to illustrate the utility of some of its principles by way of such ordinary examples as television commercial claims, a tenth grader's equivocal argument that all news is propaganda, a newspaper editorial claiming desegregation efforts have failed, and test reliability claims. His list of the characteristics of good practical thinking are more like rules of thumb than formal rules of logic. They lend themselves readily to direct application. For instance, in his advice on evaluating any person's authoritative-sounding statements he urges us to consider such things as the person's range of relevant experience, lack of conflict of interest, reputation for being honest, and care in making the statement, and whether the statement conflicts with what we otherwise have good reason to believe.

His prescription of principles to increase proficiency in thinking go beyond evaluating authoritative-sounding pronouncements to include evaluation of deductive and material reasoning, reason-giving explanations, definitions, and value statements. He also describes proficiency in observing, in inferring, or in just seeing the point in a line of reasoning, in detecting a variety of problems and taking appropriate action, in operating with a suppositional framework, and in offering a well-organized, well-formulated line of reasoning.

He characterizes the rational thinker as one who

> develops the tendencies to try to do all of the above things well, to take into account the total situation, to demand as much precision as the subject matter permits, to consider seriously other points of view than one's own, to deal in an orderly fashion with the parts of a complex situation, to seek to have one's judgement well-informed, to withhold judgement given insufficient evidence or reasons, to take or change one's position given sufficient reason and to accept the necessity of employing informed judgement.

Ennis ends with the plea that this extended conception of rational thinking "become more deliberately part of the content of general education and that it become more explicitly and fully part of the process of teaching, evaluation, research, administration, and policy setting."

Clive Beck, professor of philosophy of education at The Ontario Institute for Studies in Education, argues in his chapter that the study of ethics is an essential basis for arriving at a sound approach to values education. His basic assumption is that the serious values educator ignores traditional ethics, contemporary ethical theories, and alternative views of moral education at his peril.

Beck begins his essay with a brief tracing of various twentieth-century conceptions of moral education from ideas like "character building" and developing of the strength of will to do what is good to "critical open value inquiry" and developing the cognitive skills to decide what is good in problematic situations. He then turns to a critical examination of four recent approaches to values education. He believes that the "reasoning skills" approach, which aims at teaching useful methods for resolving values issues, is too narrow and limited a view because it does not concern itself with teaching substantive values per se. The "dilemma discussion" approach also is too narrow a view because it suggests that most values problems are of the dilemma type, and they are not. The "value clarification" approach, he argues, puts too much emphasis on the individual's arrival at personal values without recognizing that "values can be objectively good or bad, sound or unsound, that one can make a mistake in values matters." The idea that "morality is caught, not taught" is reflected in the "school organization and atmosphere" approach. While Beck notes that this view like the others picks out an important element in what constitutes values education, he also sees it as narrow and limited.

His own "reflective" approach attempts a more comprehensive view utilizing the sound insights of these other approaches plus perspectives gained from philosophical ethics. It is based on the belief that in *principle* values issues are entirely open, but in *practice* we can identify basic human values—survival, happiness, friendship, self-respect, and so forth, in light of which specific values decisions can be made. Values education in public schools in a pluralistic society thus is feasible because we do share such a common set of basic human values. Beck's program for reflective values education has three elements: (1) values inquiry resulting in the identification and refinement of basic human values, (2) the assessment and development of specific and intermediate range values, and (3) the development of emotions, attitudes, and behavior patterns that accord with the values established through values inquiry. His pedagogical discussion then turns to description of three compatible approaches and a variety of strategies for carrying out a program of reflective values education. The chapter ends with a thorough discussion of the philosophical roots of the reflective approach, tracing the relevant views of Aristotle, Hobbes, Bentham, John Dewey, and Morris Ginsberg, and grounding his views in the rich tradition of philosophical ethics.

Justice, the just society, equality, fairness, and human dignity have been central topics in Western social and political philosophy. These ideas come together in educational practice as policies for desegregation and integration are formed and acted on in contemporary America. In his chapter, Professor Kenneth A. Strike of Cornell University reflects on the landmark Supreme Court decision of 1953, *Brown* v. *Board of Education*, the relevant sociological contribution of James Coleman and Kenneth Clark, subsequent legal decisions regarding desegregation, and John Rawls's theory of justice in order to develop a moral theory of desegregation useful in the guidance of educational policymaking.

He finds two different moral theories about the evils of segregation implicit in the legal and social science literature. The first, the dominant one in the sociological literature, views segregation as wrong because it results in the unequal distribution of social goods. The moral point of school desegregation, therefore, is to provide the basis for a fair distribution of those school resources that have an effect on achievement and income. This in turn requires knowledge of the relations between such variables as race, schooling, achievement, and income as well as effective policies for racial integration that will produce the required just distribution of social goods.

The judicial community on the other hand tends to view segregation as evil because it violates the principles of "equal humanity of persons," placing on blacks the stigma of inferiority, of being less human and less worthy of respect than whites. Their remedy does not require a fairer distribution of anything except respect for the essential human dignity of persons, which must be reflected in the social order in general and in schools in particular by the eradication of anything that suggests racial disparagement or inferiority.

Such different views can and do lead to different desegregation policies and judgments. Strike uses the 1974 *Milliken* v. *Bradley* case to aptly illustrate this. The plaintiffs sought an interdistrict remedy for desegregation in Detroit, a city whose single school district was overwhelmingly black, arguing that achieving a plausible racial balance within Detroit was impossible. The Federal District Court, much influenced by social science evidence concerning the beneficial effects of racial balance on the achievement of black children, granted such a remedy, which in effect constituted a super school district of Detroit and its nearby, predominantly white suburbs. The Supreme Court, however, rejected this remedy, ordering instead a Detroit-only desegregation plan, arguing that since the suburbs had not been shown to have been involved in producing segregation in Detroit they should not be required to be involved in producing a remedy. The desegregation plan that resulted focused on eliminating the vestiges of a dual school system by ridding it of identifiably white schools and thereby created a system in which every school is predominantly black.

Strike demonstrates that these two moral positions are related in a very basic way. Theories of distributive justice, he argues, must assume a principle of equal humanity of persons and equal consideration of an individual's interest regardless of how persons may differ from one another. Differences in the distribution of social goods cannot be justified on the basis of irrelevant personal characteristics without violating the principle of equal humanity of persons. The subjective side of this principle is self-respect, knowing that you as an individual are worth as much as any other individual. One cannot have self-respect if the distribution of social goods is fundamentally unfair. Strike concludes:

> What these arguments indicate, then, is that the two moral theories imply one another and that when separated give an incomplete view of what is at stake in issues of segregation and desegregation. If we start with a theory that views segregation as noxious primarily because it maligns the humanity of Blacks, we are soon led to a concern for how schools affect the fair distribution of social goods. For the failure to equitably distribute economic goods on a criterion of race is a way of maligning the full humanity of Blacks. If, on the other hand, we start with a concern for the fair distribution of even purely economic goods, we are led to a concern for self respect and thereby to a recognition that the affirmation of the dignity and worth of all in our public educational policy is a fundamental consideration. . . . This larger view requires us to get our policy making act together.

Since the publication of Thomas S. Kuhn's *The Structure of Scientific Revolutions* (1962), there has been renewed attention in history and philosophy of science to the *dynamics* of science: how scientists engaged in a research program deal with recalcitrant phenomena, how people in rival frameworks or paradigms communicate with each other, how changes in theories come about and how can it be determined if a new theory constitutes an improvement. Many of these issues are pertinent for educational researchers, or for those who wish to use well-grounded research results as a basis for shaping educational policy. D. C. Phillips, professor of education at Stanford University, sketches some of the current views in philosophy of science and provides fruitful applications of the philosophical perspective gained to education.

One of the major problems dealt with concerns the possible "incommensurability of paradigms," the claim that different theories represent completely different worlds and are in fact different languages, so completely different from each other that one cannot "measure" or evaluate claims in one paradigm from the perspective of the other paradigm. Given that the field of educational practice and research is replete with rival theories and contrasting approaches, it is not clear in many cases whether these are conflicting or complementary. How is the nonexpert practitioner or policymaker to decide?

> Even the normally sedate field of history of education has been shaken by the work of the so called revisionists; educational psychology is the home of the Skinnerians, information-processing theorists, social learning theorists, Ericksonians, Rogerians, Piagetians, and Freudians; and in sociology of education the descendants of the functionalists face up to the neo-Marxists, symbolic interactionists, and sociobiologists.

Reflections on the nature of science and the validity of scientific claims, especially in light of the work of Lakatos, Toulmin, and Feyerabend, leads Phillips to assert that

> although there is little overall unanimity, . . . contemporary philosophy of science does emphasize the importance of research programs progressively opening-up new phenomena, the exposing of assumptions, and the giving and receiving of strong criticism. . . . And if full justice is to be done to educational research, then some way must be found to incorporate evaluation of the ongoing stream of work plus the basic theoretical orientation that has inspired it.

He turns to Lakatos's view of research programs evolving over time, either progressing or degenerating, and points to the relevance of this view in assessing educational research in general and, by way of example, the research of Arthur Jensen on race and IQ and that of Lawrence Kohlberg on moral development. The discussion clearly demonstrates the value of philosophical perspective for educators who both produce and consume scientific knowledge.

The perspective of metaphysics is taken up by Professor James E. McClellan of the State University of New York–Albany in the last chapter, which is on "first philosophy." In a philosophical tradition not as popular today as it once was, McClellan asks what happens when you push the basic questions of life and education back to bedrock. What is real? What is truth? What are human beings? What is learning? Why educate? We are asked not to settle for answers until no more meaningful questions can be asked. We are asked to do first philosophy. Any theory of human values and education, he argues, must be grounded in a comprehensive theory of the world. The theory of the world McClellan finds most plausible is "materialism."

"What is a material object?" he asks.

> It's one of the things that this universe contains. How do we know? Because the physical theory that makes it possible for billions of human beings to exist on the surface of this planet commits us to the existence of such entities. . . . But why is our universe so ordered? Now you've stepped from philosophical bedrock into the abyss of idle speculation. First philosophy requires we stop here.

His subsequent arguments are aimed at demonstrating that there is a materialistic continuum of all things we take to be real including intangibles and abstractions. Through the advances of science, we are understanding more and more that human beings are also physical entities with complex energy-exchange systems interacting with other physical objects in a tight binding of beings to beings and being to world. Our material evolution in the world includes the development of language and rationality. We are complex physical objects.

> What difference does it make for our practice work as educators when we fully and consciously accept the first philosophy to which we are already committed by our mode of material existence? The fact is that from those points of bedrock one *cannot* move by logically necessary steps to any particular, practical conclusion. That's what materialism entails. One can test one's arguments [via first philosophy] to see whether they involve knowing things that aren't real. Once you get the hang of it you can easily spot the unreality in most of the talk coming from the purveyors of existentialism, phenomenology, astrology, psychology, and such like. . . . One is impelled by first philosophy to join the revolutionary movement. . . . More immediately, one who accepts a materialist first philosophy is impelled to look upon children, all children, as the smartest little animals in the kingdom, impelled to want to help them get responsible

control over their own wants and beliefs, to join with them in creating a new world. . . . When all the illusions have been blown away, we human beings are but wanting, believing, language using animals. Given the objective, material realities, what do we want for ourselves and our children? . . . How can we help those coming to maturity achieve the skills and maturity required for being *collectively* intelligent [in getting what's wanted]? If one can answer those questions from the standpoint of a materialist's first philosophy without being impelled toward a revolutionary political commitment, please show me how.

The yearbook ends on this philosophically quizzical note.

III

We come now to a discussion of the relationship between philosophy of education and the education of professional educators. It would be inappropriate, I believe, to think of the organization of the NSSE yearbook as *the* mode of delivery of philosophy of education to educators. Even though its organization by way of subareas of philosophy does reflect what philosophy of education is about, it does not mirror it, that is, provide an exact image of what all philosophers of education do, nor does it present the only topics of educational interest in each subarea. Therefore, it should not be adopted wholesale as the structure for *the* course in philosophy of education at any institution. That would be to totally misread its usefulness. It would also be wrong to view this structure as the justification for a series of courses in each of the subareas of philosophy to be required of all educators. Nevertheless, the structure does speak in a very general way to the role philosophy can play in the proper education of the professional educator and to a new view of educational "foundations," which I will now briefly sketch.

In speaking generally about the education of educators, I will not deal with two obvious components of professional education: first, the liberal education base necessary to insure that any educator is an educated person, and second, the special knowledge of one's subject matter if one is to be an effective teacher. Rather, I will deal with the third broad knowledge component, which I will call professional knowledge. The very concept of *profession* carries with it the idea of highly refined and knowledgeable skill in use for human service. Obviously, such skill can be acquired only through practice; but that practice must be critically informed by substantive knowledge and used with the sensitive application of standards of professional and ethical judgment. The substantive professional knowledge required is of two types—*knowledge of professional practices* and *disciplinary knowledge* of relevant educational phenomena. An example of the first would be knowledge of methods for teaching foreign languages or knowledge of interviewing techniques for guidance counselors. Examples of the second would be knowledge of the economics of education for administrators and knowledge of the effects of culture on learning for teachers in bilingual education programs. I will be dealing only with the latter.

I think it is important to recognize that the old idea of social, philosophical, and psychological foundations as represented by general knowledge in the disciplines and supposedly offering something of common importance to all educators is quite different from the idea of a new foundations that is primarily aimed at informing specialized professional practice. This does not mean that there should be no common core of experience for educators, which the older foundations sought to provide. In fact, where entry into the profession is ordinarily based on preparation for teaching by undergraduates, I think it is important to find ways to provide initiates with a common base of general knowledge about their chosen field. However, since so many teachers are required and others do continue their professional education at least through the master's level and since so many individuals may not enter the profession until reaching the graduate level, we need to think of ways to integrate the specialized knowledge available in the disciplines with the increasing professional specialization sought after in this longer course of study.

While I think it is possible to sketch the new foundations whole and describe the place of history, psychology, and the social sciences as well as philosophy in such a sketch, I will limit my description of the new foundations to the role that philosophy of education might play in it with both its general and specialized offerings. I would like to argue that graduate education, even on the master's level, ought to be considered as specialized education. And I would like to argue that philosophy of education as well as other discipline-based studies can and should provide specialized knowledge directly relevant to the educational specialists. This runs counter to most of current practice, which ordinarily requires some foundations work of a general sort on the undergraduate level and then repetitiously requires additional general courses in foundations of education on the master's level. Some philosophers feel that you cannot do specialized work in one of the subareas of philosophy unless you have done some general work in philosophy. I do not believe that this is so. I think that soundly educated teachers of literature who have completed undergraduate work with or without philosophy and taught for a few years can move directly into a course in aesthetics or the philosophy of literature taught by a philosopher of education sensitive to their problems and gain much of relevance to their conception of teaching. The same also would hold true for philosophy of science for science teachers, philosophy of language for the teachers of foreign languages, philosophy of history for historians, and so forth.

But I also believe that there is important general philosophical work of two sorts to be done on the undergraduate level. It is unfortunate that the diversified work that has gone on in philosophy of education over the last twenty-five years has led to a neglect of the rich tradition of educational thought to which all who would call themselves educators ought to have some exposure. The fault has not been so much with the philosophers as with the archaic idea that one general course in philosophy of education (no matter what topics it might deal with) is all that prospective teachers need to become properly philosophical about their professional practice. With such a rich set of ideas, topics, and problems that scholarly philosophers of education have generated in the last quarter of a century, it is no wonder that they felt it important to include many of these in their basic course. Unfortunately, what gave way in many cases was traditional thought, which so frequently students merely regurgitated anyway, and in its place were put lively topics and problems that stimulated genuine philosophical thought. I hope we would agree as philosophers and educators that a meaningful engagement of the minds of undergraduate preprofessionals with traditional educational thought on aims, purposes, curriculum, teaching, and learning as developed by great minds like Plato, Rousseau, Whitehead, and Dewey and by serious contemporary public philosophers of education should be part of a professional's education no matter what else philosophers have to offer. One should come to these basic ideas at an early stage in one's professional preparation with a pedagogical attitude of romance as described by Whitehead as the exciting first stage of engagement with some subject that leads to embracing it with love and caring. One should ground oneself in one's profession by sharing attempts by great and concerned thinkers to make sense of education and its public purposes. Such study should not be technically philosophical but only be the start on a lifelong undertaking to try to make education as one's calling more meaningful.

There is one other thing that would be extremely important for philosophers to provide on the undergraduate level, and here I am calling for a second and more technical course in philosophy for all educators at this stage in their professional development. Philosophers care about straight thinking and are especially well equipped to teach people how to do it. Educators should be the guardians of reasonableness and sound thinking no matter what their professional specialization. Putting these two ideas together recommends philosophical teaching at the undergraduate level directed at providing skill in practical reasoning and conceptual analysis and the motivation to teach and insist on sound thinking in every classroom on every level of education. Such a skills course should be quite different from a content course dealing with classical and contemporary ideas about aims, purposes, curricula, teaching, and learning. But both are important contributions philosophy can make to the undergraduate preservice preparation of professionals.

After some experience in the field, those who return to graduate school to continue developing in their specialized teaching field should not have to repeat the kind of philosophical work that was relevant to their undergraduate career. They should have the opportunity to pursue specialized knowledge in philosophy as well as in other areas of the graduate curriculum that would most directly inform their practice. Here, for those who will continue teaching a special subject, the easiest and most relevant part of philosophy to their work, as I have already argued, is the philosophy of some subject. While there is a philosophy of science, of language, of history, of mathematics, unfortunately there is no philosophy of business education, geography, health education, physical education, nutrition, and so forth; nor do I think that the suggestion should give license to inventing such philosophies. However, it would not be inappropriate to think of developing *some* new areas; for instance, for the elementary teacher, work in the philosophy of children's rights and the concept of childhood might be quite appropriate. But if no sound philosophical study is available and relevant to a specialized area of teaching, then sensible educators ought to be the first not to require philosophy of such master's candidates.

But what of those who shift directions in their graduate work after either completing undergraduate preparation in education or coming to education anew on the graduate level? What of those who seek specialized education to become administrators, supervisors, educational technologists, reading specialists, guidance counselors, school psychologists? For those new to the profession at the graduate level, we should consider to what extent the basic philosophical work in straight thinking and classical-contemporary educational thought ought to be provided. But for all others, and for those newcomers, we should be concerned predominantly with the philosophical study most relevant to their specializations. One could try to argue that curriculum specialists should know epistemology or that administrators would benefit most from work in social and political theory. But I think that this tack is inappropriate. The match attempts to be too neat and the world just is not made that way. Rather, I think that more mature students, especially those with work experience, should be able to bring their own best judgment and genuine search for philosophical perspective to choices among courses in philosophy of education offered in such subareas of philosophy as ethics, social and political philosophy, epistemology, theory of mind, philosophical psychology, and so forth. They should be able to bring from their personal experience as practicing professionals sets of special philosophical concerns that they feel need addressing in their continuing education as professionals. Concerns with ethnics or moral education need not be confined to the continuing teacher or to the administrator or curriculum planner. Ethics and education would be a proper study for the guidance counselor who may see the need to wrestle with professional ethical problems of the morality of guiding peoples' life choices. To provide the opportunity for professional educators to pursue their special and deepest philosophical concerns ought to be the aim of philosophy of education at the graduate level.

At this point, potential high costs and proliferation of courses may seem to lead inevitably to the failure of my proposals. But the economics of such a scheme for a new foundations concept of philosophy of education is not necessarily what it first seems to be. At first one might expect the multiplication of special courses in a number of subareas to require considerable additional staffing. That might be desirable, but it is not necessarily required. If one considers a modest-sized institution of, say, two thousand undergraduate and graduate students combined, and if each student were required to take one course in philosophy of education, then ten courses averaging twenty students per course would have to be staffed and taught. If two courses were required on the undergraduate level, one in effective thinking and one in educational thought as proposed, that would still provide for eight courses in the subareas of philosophy and education to be taught on the graduate level. Granted the undergraduate courses would of necessity be large and the graduate courses small, still instead of two instructors teaching ten courses in philosophy of education as a general subject, they could teach a variety of courses in philosophy of education that have more direct relevance to the preprofessional and to the practicing educator. Of course, richer offerings and smaller classes would be possible if economic considerations were not primary.

I have said little about the other traditional foundations areas, but it seems to me that the general idea of providing very basic work in history, psychology, and the social sciences of education at the undergraduate level should be followed on the master's level with an opportunity for the educational specialists to benefit from the subareas of specialization within any of those disciplines. Thus, for example, the school administrator should be able to study the sociology of organizations and the guidance counselor, the sociology of occupations. Such examples could easily be multiplied across the various disciplines and specializations. The most difficult problems in reformulating a new foundations curriculum along such lines would be to avoid multiplying subspecializations *ad infinitum* with a one-to-one correspondence to each and every esoteric educational specialization, and finding sensible ways to cluster similar educational specializations with the shared need for knowledge of certain disciplinary subareas. But solving such problems is unfortunately well beyond the scope of this article.

IV

It remains but to sketch out what the education of a philo   ıer of education ought to look like if the basic ideas in this essay   sound. First, it should be obvious that for doctoral work, a str ₁g undergraduate preparation in philosophy is essential. There is no way to become broadly conversant with the multiple subareas of philosophical inquiry overnight or in a year or two of graduate study in a school of education.[4] But it is equally essential for anyone who would philosophize effectively·about education to become directly conversant with some mode of educational practice. Indeed, we could increase the potential for philosophical contributions to specialized educational practice to the degree to which we could bring young philosophers to know what educators actually do, how they think, and what philosophical dimensions their specialized work has.

Given these two assumptions about the need for a sound knowledge of both philosophy and educational practice, I believe that the following would provide the essential components for an effective doctoral program in philosophy of education at this stage of the development of the field:

1. *Subareas of Philosophy* Advanced study in the subareas of philosophy with an eye to mastering the contemporary philosophical literature of at least three subareas for subsequent development as special areas of educational concern.

2. *Subareas of Philosophy and Education* Advanced studies in philosophy of education that utilize the subareas of philosophy to illuminate educational topics.

3. *Curriculum Theory and Pedagogical Theory* Study of classical and contemporary philosophical thought on curriculum and teaching with an emphasis on continuing the philosophical research tradition in these areas.

4. *Public Philosophies of Education* Study of major historical and contemporary views on education writ large as a social institution with an eye to developing ways to meaningfully introduce the preservice student to this basic philosophical dimension of their professional life.

5. *Philosophical Thinking* Study of formal and informal logic, practical reasoning, and the skills and techniques of philosophical inquiry. This should provide for both the honing of the tools of the philosopher-scholar and developing insight into the ways of teaching sound thinking skills to educators.

6. *Knowledge of Educational Practice* Study, training, and gaining familiarity with some mode of specialized educational practice like the teaching of a subject or of a grade level, counseling, administering, and so forth, to insure that philosophers of education will have some firsthand knowledge of some aspect of the phenomena they would philosophize about.

7. *Demonstration of Scholarly and Professional Proficiency* Besides the scholarly dissertation that demonstrates mastery of the technical skills of the philosopher, philosophers of education should also demonstrate their ability to philosophically treat a topic in a way comprehensible to the professional educator. This might be done by the dissertation itself, by providing a professional version of it to be examined by a committee of professors of education, by publishing an article in a professional journal, and so forth.

I am sure there is more of worth in both substance and procedure to specify for the sound education of future professional philosophers of education, but I will stop here. This essay has tried to do too many things already. But if it has only helped to reset the expectations of educators with regard to what philosophy of education in both its public and professional senses has to offer them, then it has accomplished its major purpose and paved the way for an intelligent reading and use of the eightieth NSSE yearbook.

Footnotes

1 I absolve my philosophial colleagues involved with me in the NSSE project from responsibility for any of the peripheral ideas about educating educators or philosophers presented here while I also take this opportunity to thank them for their contributions to the yearbook from which I drew freely in the central section of this article describing each chapter.

2 See "Preface," my introduction to this book, which distinguishes philosophy of education in its broad public sense from a narrower professional sense.

3 This and all following quotations from chapters in the yearbook cannot be given proper citation because, at this writing, final drafts of chapters are not yet available. I have tried to present each author's view accurately and I have taken the liberty to paraphrase rough drafts extensively, but I assume the responsibility for any misrepresentation of what any of the authors' final drafts actually say.

4 This obvious requirement, however, ought not to stand in the way of doctoral study for those educators without a philosophical background who became genuinely interested in curriculum theory, theory of pedagogy, and philosophy of education primarily in its public sense. A sound doctoral degree program in "educational theory," located perhaps in curriculum and teaching but jointly planned and taught with the philosophy of education faculty, could provide the requisite mastery of the literature in these areas and the skills needed to deal with them in a scholarly fashion.

Index

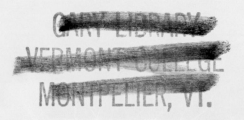